Edward James Corbett (1875-1955), popularly known as **Jim Corbett** was an army officer of the Colonel rank in the British-Indian Army and later he turned as a nature conservationist, wildlife lover, and a revered author. He was born in Nainital. Since his childhood, he has a deep fascination for the forests and wildlife, and due to his interest in wildlife, he became a good tracker and hunter with time. Due to his amazing skill of tracking and hunting, he was often sought after by the then government of the united province to track and kill the tiger and leopard who becomes a man-eater. Even though he was the skilled hunter, he never killed any wild animal other than man-eaters.

After many years as a celebrated hunter, he then developed a hobby of wildlife photography, especially, recording films of tigers in their natural habitat. He also used to give lectures on the rich natural heritage of India and the importance of the conservation of forests and wildlife to the school students. He also penned his experience as a hunter and written many books on wildlife and hunting experiences. His most famous book was Man-Eaters of Kumaon that intensely portrayed his own hunting adventures.

Later in his life, Jim Corbett started a movement to conserve the wild animals and forests. He also used his influence over the provincial government and lead the path that cleared the establishment of the first national park in India, the Hailey National Park, in 1930s. The name later changed to the Jim Corbett National Park after the independence of India in 1957 in the honor of the legendary Jim Corbett.

MAN-EATERS OF
KUMAON

Jim Corbett

MAN-EATERS OF KUMAON
by Jim Corbett

This edition first published in 2019

Published in India by:
Embassy Book Distributors
120, Great Western Building,
Maharashtra Chamber of Commerce Lane,
Fort, Mumbai - 400 023.
Tel : (91-22) 22819546 / 22818567.
Email : info@embassybooks.in
Website : www.embassybooks.in

Distribution Centres:
Mumbai, Bangalore, Kolkata, Chennai,
Hyderabad, New Delhi, Pune

No part of this book may be reproduced, stored in a retrieval system, or transmitted by any means, electronic mechanical, photocopying, recording, or otherwise, without written permission from the copyright holder.

ISBN: 978-93-88247-29-0

Page Design and Layout by PSV Kumarasamy

CONTENTS

Author's Note 7

The Champawat Man-eater....................................17

Robin..51

The Chowgarh Tigers..67

The Bachelor of Powalgarh 131

The Mohan Man-eater...149

The Fish of My Dreams 187

The Kanda Man-eater 197

The Pipal Pani Tiger...215

The Thak Man-eater 229

AUTHOR'S NOTE

As many of the stories in this book are about man-eating tigers, it is perhaps desirable to explain why these animals develop man-eating tendencies.

A man-eating tiger is a tiger that has been compelled, through stress of circumstances beyond its control, to adopt a diet alien to it. The stress of circumstances is, in nine cases out of ten, wounds, and in the tenth case old age. The wound that has caused a particular tiger to take to man-eating might be the result of a carelessly fired shot and failure to follow up and recover the wounded animal, or be the result of the tiger having lost its temper when killing a porcupine. Human beings are not the natural prey of tigers, and it is only when tigers have been incapacitated through wounds or old age that, in order to live, they are compelled to take to a diet of human flesh.

A tiger when killing its natural prey, which it does either by stalking or lying in wait for it, depends for the success of its attack on its speed and, to a lesser extent, on the condition of its teeth and claws. When, therefore, a tiger is suffering from one or more painful wounds, or when its teeth are missing or defective and its claws worn down, and it is unable to catch the animals it has been accustomed to eating, it is driven by necessity to killing human beings. The change-over from animal to human flesh is, I believe, in most cases accidental. As an illustration of what I mean by 'accidental' I quote the case of the Muktesar man-eating tigress. This tigress, a comparatively young animal, in an encounter with a porcupine lost an eye and got some fifty quills, varying in length from one to nine inches, embedded in the arm and under the pad of her right foreleg. Several of these quills after striking a bone had doubled back in the form of a U, the point and the broken-off end being quite close together. Suppurating sores formed where she endeavoured to extract the quills with her teeth, and while she was lying up in a thick patch of grass, starving and licking her wounds, a woman selected this particular patch of grass to cut as fodder for her cattle. At first the tigress took no notice, but when the woman had cut the grass right up to where she was lying the tigress struck once, the blow crushing in the woman's skull. Death was instantaneous, for, when found the following day, she was grasping her sickle with one hand and holding a tuft of grass, which she was about to cut when struck, with the other. Leaving the woman lying where she had fallen, the tigress limped off for a distance of over a mile and took refuge in a little hollow under a fallen tree. Two days later a man came to chip fire-wood off this fallen tree, and the tigress who was lying on the far side killed him. The man fell across the tree and, as he had removed his coat and shirt and the tigress had clawed his back when killing him:, it is possible that the smell of the blood trickling down his body as he hung across the bole of the tree first gave her the idea that he was something that she could satisfy her hunger with. However that may be, before leaving him she ate a small portion from his back. A day later she killed her third victim deliberately, and without having received any provocation. Thereafter she became an established man-eater and had killed twenty-four people before she was finally accounted for.

A tiger on a fresh kill, or a wounded tiger, or a tigress with small cubs will occasionally kill human beings who disturb them; but these tigers cannot, by any stretch of imagination, be called man-eaters, though they are often so called. Personally I would give a tiger the benefit of the doubt once, and once again, before classing it as a man-eater, and whenever possible I would subject the alleged victim to a post-mortem before letting the kill go down on the records as the kill of a tiger or a leopard, as the case might be. This subject of post-mortems of human beings alleged to have been killed by either tigers or leopards or, in the plains, by wolves or hyenas, is of great importance, for, though I refrain from giving instances, I know of cases where deaths have wrongly been ascribed to carnivora.

It is a popular fallacy that all man-eaters are old and mangy, the mange being attributed to the excess of salt in human flesh. I am not competent to give any opinion on the relative quantity of salt in human or animal flesh; but I can, and I do, assert that a diet of human flesh, so far from having an injurious effect on the coat of man-eaters, has quite the opposite effect, for all the man-eaters I have seen have had remarkably fine coats.

Another popular belief in connection with man-eaters is that the cubs of these animals automatically become man-eaters. This is quite a reasonable supposition; but it is not borne out by actual facts, and the reason why the cubs of a man-eater do not themselves become man-eaters is that human beings are not the natural prey of tigers, or of leopards.

A cub will eat whatever its mother provides, and I have even known of tiger cubs assisting their mothers to kill human beings; but I do not know of a single instance of a cub, after it had left the protection of its parent, or after that parent had been killed, taking to killing human beings.

In the case of human beings killed by carnivora, the doubt is often expressed as to whether the animal responsible for the kill is a tiger or leopard. As a general rule – to which I have seen no exceptions – tigers are responsible for all kills that take place in daylight, and leopards are responsible for all kills that take place in the dark. Both animals are semi-nocturnal forest-dwellers, have much the same habits, employ similar methods of killing, and both are capable of carrying their human victims for long distances. It would be natural, therefore, to expect them to hunt at the same hours; and that they do not do so is due to the difference in courage of the two animals. When a tiger becomes a man-eater it loses all fear of human beings and, as human beings move about more freely in the day than they do at night, it is able to secure its victims during daylight hours and there is no necessity for it to visit their habitations at night. A leopard on the other hand, even after it has killed scores of human beings, never loses its fear of man; and, as it is unwilling to face up to human beings in daylight, it secures its victims when they are moving about at night, or by breaking into their houses at night. Owing to these characteristics of the two animals, namely, that one loses its fear of human beings and kills in the daylight, while the other retains its fear and kills in the dark, man-eating tigers are easier to shoot than man-eating leopards.

The frequency with which a man-eating tiger kills depends on: (a) the supply of natural food in the area in which it is operating; (b) the nature of the disability which has caused it to become a man-eater; and (c) whether 1t is a male or a female with cubs.

Those of us who lack the opportunity of forming our own opinion on any particular subject are apt to accept the opinions of others, and in no case is this more apparent than in the case of tigers – here I do not refer to man-eaters in particular, but to tigers in general. The author who first used the words 'as cruel as a tiger' and 'as bloodthirsty as a tiger', when attempting to emphasize the evil character of the villain of his piece, not only showed a lamentable ignorance of the animal he defamed, but coined phrases which have come into universal circulation, and which are mainly responsible for the wrong opinion of tigers held by all except that very small proportion of the public who have the opportunity of forming their own opinions.

When I see the expression 'as cruel as a tiger' and 'as bloodthirsty as a tiger' in print, I think of a small boy armed with an old muzzle-loading gun – the right barrel of which was split for six inches of its length, and the stock and barrels of which were kept from falling apart by lashings of brass wire – wandering through the jungles of the terai and *bhabar* in the days when there were ten tigers to every one that now survives; sleeping anywhere he happened to be when night came on, with a small fire to give him company and warmth, wakened at intervals by the calling of tigers, sometimes in the distance, at other times near at hand; throwing another stick on the fire and turning over and continuing his interrupted sleep without one thought of unease; knowing from his own short experience and from what others, who like himself had spent their days in the jungles, had told him, that a tiger, unless molested, would do him no harm; or during day-light hours avoiding any tiger he saw, and when that was not possible, standing perfectly still until it had passed and gone, before continuing on his way. And I think of him on one occasion stalking half a dozen jungle fowl that were feeding in, the open, and, on creeping up to a plum-bush and standing up to peer over, the bush heaving and a tiger walking out on the far side and, on clearing the bush, turning round and looking at the boy with an expression on its face which said as clearly as any words, 'Hello, kid, what are you doing here?' and, receiving no answer, turning round and walking away very slowly without once looking back. And then again I think of the tens of thousands of men, women, and children who, while working in the forests or cutting grass or collecting dry sticks, pass day after day close to where tigers are lying up and who, when they return safely to their homes, do not even know that they have been under the observation of this so-called 'cruel' and 'bloodthirsty' animal.

Half a century has rolled by since the day the tiger walked out of the plum-bush, the latter thirty-two years of which have been spent in the more or less regular pursuit of man-eaters, and though sights have been seen which would have caused a stone to weep, I have not seen a case where a tiger has been deliberately cruel or where it has been bloodthirsty to the extent that it has killed, without provocation, more than it has needed to satisfy its hunger or the hunger of its cubs.

A tiger's function in the scheme of things is to help maintain the balance in nature and if, on rare occasions when driven by dire necessity, he kills a human being, or when his natural food has been ruthlessly exterminated by man he kills two per cent of the cattle he is alleged to have killed, it is not fair that for these acts a whole species should be branded as being cruel and bloodthirsty.

Sportsmen are admittedly conservative, the reason

being that it has taken them years to form their opinions, and as each individual has a different point of view, it is only natural that opinions should differ on minor, or even m some cases on major points, and for this reason I do not flatter myself that all the opinions I have expressed will meet with universal agreement.

There is, however, one point on which I am convinced that all sportsmen – no matter whether their point of view has been a platform on a tree, the back of an elephant, or their own feet – will agree with me, and that is, that a tiger is a large-hearted gentleman with boundless courage and that when he is exterminated – as exterminated he will be unless public opinion rallies to his support – India will be the poorer by having lost the finest of her fauna.

Leopards, unlike tigers, are to a certain extent scavengers, and become man-eaters by acquiring a taste for human flesh when unrestricted slaughter of game has deprived them of their natural food.

The dwellers in our hills are predominantly Hindu, and as such cremate their dead. The cremation invariably takes place on the bank of a stream or river in order that the ashes may be washed down into the Ganges, and eventually into the sea. As most of the villages are situated high up on the hills, while the streams or rivers are in many cases miles away down in the valleys, it will be realized that a funeral entails a considerable tax on the man-power of a small community when, in addition to the carrying party, labour has to be provided to collect and carry the fuel needed for the cremation. In normal times these rites are carried out very effectively; but when disease in epidemic form sweeps through the hills and the inhabitants die faster than they can be disposed of, a very simple rite, which consists of placing a live coal in the mouth of the deceased, is performed in the village and the body is then carried to the edge of the hill and cast into the valley below.

A leopard, in an area in which his natural food is scarce, finding these bodies very soon acquires a taste for human flesh, and when the disease dies down and normal conditions are established, he very naturally, on finding his food supply cut off, takes to killing human beings.

Of the two man-eating leopards of Kumaon, which between them killed five hundred and twenty-five human beings, one followed on the heels of a very severe outbreak of cholera, while the other followed the mysterious disease which swept through India in 1918 and was called 'war fever'.

THE CHAMPAWAT
MAN-EATER

I was shooting with Eddie Knowles in Malani when I first heard of the tiger which later received official recognition as the 'Champawat man-eater'.

Eddie, who will long be remembered in this province as a sportsman par excellence and the possessor of an inexhaustible fund of shikar yarns, was one of those few, and very fortunate, individuals who possess the best of everything in life. His rifle was without equal in accuracy and striking power, and while one of his brothers was the best gun shot in India, another brother was the best tennis player in the Indian Army. When therefore Eddie informed me that his brother-in-law, the best shikari in the world, had been deputed by the Government to shoot the Champawat man-eater, it was safe to assume that a very definite period had been put to the animal's activities.

The tiger, however, for some inexplicable reason, did not die, and was causing the Government a great deal of anxiety when I visited Naini Tal four years later. Rewards were offered, special shikaris employed, and parties of Gurkhas sent out from the depot in Almora. Yet in spite of these measures, the toll of human victims continued to mount alarmingly.

The tigress, for such the animal turned out to be, had arrived in K:umaon as a full-fledged man-eater, from Nepal, whence she had been driven out by a body of armed Nepalese after she had killed two hundred human beings, and during the four years she had been operating in Kumaon had added two hundred and thirty-four to this number.

This is how matters stood when shortly after my arrival in Naini Tal I received a visit from Berthoud. Berthoud, who was Deputy Commissioner of Naini Tal at that time, and who after his tragic death now lies buried in an obscure grave in Haldwani, was a man who was loved and respected by all who knew him, and it is not surprising therefore that when he told me of the trouble the man-eater was giving the people of his district, and the anxiety it was causing him, he took my promise with him that I would start for Champawat immediately on receipt of news of the next human kill.

Two conditions I made, however: one that the Government rewards be cancelled, and the other, that the special shikaris, and regulars from Almora, be withdrawn. My reasons for making these conditions need no explanation, for I am sure all sportsmen share my aversion to being classed as a reward-hunter and are as anxious as I am to avoid the risk of being accidentally shot. These conditions were agreed to, and a week later Berthoud paid me an early morning visit and informed me that news had been brought in during the night by runners that a woman had been killed by the man-eater at Pali, a village between Dabidhura and Dhunaghat.

In anticipation of a start at short notice, I had engaged six men to carry my camp-kit, and leaving after break-fast, we did a march the first day of seventeen miles to Dhari. Breakfasting at Mornaula next morning, we spent the night at Dabidhura, and arrived at Pali the following evening, five days after the woman had been killed.

The people of the village, numbering some fifty men, women, and children, were in a state of abject terror, and though the sun was still up when I arrived I found the entire population inside their homes behind locked doors, and it was not until my men had made a fire in the courtyard and I was sitting down to a cup of tea that a door here and there was cautiously opened, and the frightened inmates emerged.

I was informed that for five days no one had gone beyond their own doorsteps – the insanitary condition of the courtyard testified to the truth of this statement – that food was running short, and that the people would starve if the tiger was not killed or driven away.

That the tiger was still in the vicinity was apparent. For three nights it had been heard calling on the road, distant a hundred yards from the houses, and that very day it had been seen on the cultivated land at the lower end of the village.

The Headman of the village very willingly placed a room at my disposal, but as there were eight of us to share it, and the only door it possessed opened on to the insanitary courtyard, I elected to spend the night in the open.

After a scratch meal which had to do duty for dinner, I saw my men safely shut into the room and myself took up a position on the side of the road, with my back to a tree. The villagers said the tiger was in the habit of perambulating along this road, and as the moon was at the full I thought there was a chance of my getting a shot – provided I saw it first.

I had spent many nights in the jungle looking for game, but this was the first time I had ever spent a night looking for a man-eater. The length of road immediately in front of me was brilliantly lit by the moon, but to right and left the overhanging trees cast dark shadows, and when the night wind agitated the branches and the shadows moved, I saw a dozen tigers advancing on me, and bitterly regretted the impulse that had induced me to place myself at the man-eater's mercy. I lacked the courage to return to the village and admit I was too frightened to carry out my self-imposed task, and with teeth chattering, as much from fear as from cold, I sat out the Jong night. As the grey dawn was lighting up the snowy range which I was facing, I rested my head on my drawn-up knees, and it was in this position my men an hour later found me – fast asleep; of the tiger I had neither heard nor seen anything.

Back in the village I tried to get the men – who I could see were very surprised I had survived the night – to take me to the places where the people of the village had from time to time been killed, but this they were unwilling to do. From the courtyard they pointed out the direction in which the kills had taken place; the last kill – the one that had brought me to the spot – I was told, had taken place round the shoulder of the hill to the west of the village. The women and girls, some twenty in number, who had been out collecting oak-leaves for the cattle when the unfortunate woman had been killed, were eager to give me details of the occurrence. It appeared that the party had set out two hours before midday and, after going half a mile, had climbed into trees to cut leaves. The victim and two other women had selected a tree growing on the edge of a ravine, which I subsequently found was about four feet deep and ten to twelve feet wide. Having cut all the leaves she needed, the woman was climbing down from the tree when the tiger, who had approached unseen, stood up on its hind legs and caught her by the foot. Her hold was torn from the branch she was letting herself down by, and, pulling her into the ravine, the tiger released her foot, and while she was struggling to rise caught her by the throat. After killing her it sprang up the side of the ravine and disappeared with her into some heavy undergrowth.

All this had taken place a few feet from the two women on the tree, and had been witnessed by the entire party. As soon as the tiger and its victim were out of sight, the terror-stricken women and girls ran back to the village. The men had just come in for their midday meal and, when all were assembled and armed with drums, metal cooking-pots – anything in fact that would produce a noise – the rescue party set off, the men leading and the women bringing up the rear.

Arrived at the ravine in which the woman had been killed, the very important question of 'what next?' was being debated when the tiger interrupted the proceedings by emitting a loud roar from the bushes thirty yards away. As one man, the party turned and fled helter-skelter back to the village. When breath had been regained, accusations were made against one and another of having been the first to run and cause the stampede. Words ran high until it was suggested that if no one was afraid and all were as brave as they claimed to be, why not go back and rescue the woman without loss of more time? The suggestion was adopted, and three times the party got as far as the ravine. On the third occasion the one man who was armed with a gun fired it off, and brought the tiger roaring out of the bushes; after this the attempted rescue was very wisely abandoned. On my asking the gun man why he had not discharged his piece into the bushes instead of up into the air, he said the tiger was already greatly enraged and that if by any mischance he had hit it, it would undoubtedly have killed him.

For three hours that morning I walked round the

village looking for tracks and hoping, and at the same time dreading, •to meet the tiger. At one place in a dark heavily wooded ravine, while I was skirting some bushes, a covey of kaleege pheasants fluttered screaming out of them, and I thought my heart had stopped beating for good.

My men had cleared a spot under a walnut-tree for my meals, and after breakfast the Headman of the village asked me to mount guard while the wheat crop was being cut. He said that if the crop was not harvested in my presence, it would not be harvested at all, for the people were too frightened to leave their homes. Half an hour later the entire population of the village, assisted by my men, were hard at work while I stood on guard with a loaded rifle. By evening the crop from five large fields had been gathered, leaving only two small patches close to the houses, which the Headman said he would have no difficulty in dealing with the next day.

The sanitary condition of the village had been much improved, and a second room for my exclusive use placed at my disposal; and that night, with thorn bushes securely wedged in the doorway to admit ventilation and exclude the man-cater, I made up for the sleep l had lost the previous night.

My presence was beginning to put new heart into the people, and they were moving about more freely, but I had not yet gained sufficient of their confidence to renew my request to be shown round the jungle, to which I attached some importance. These people knew every foot of the ground for miles round, and could, if they wished, show me where I was most likely to find the tiger, or in any case, where I could see its pug-marks. That the man-eater was a tiger was an established fact, but it was not known whether the animal was young or old, a male or a female, and this information, which I believed would help me to get in touch with it, I could only ascertain by examining its pug-marks.

After an early tea that morning I announced that I wanted meat for my men and asked the villagers if they could direct me to where I could shoot a ghooral (mountain goat). The village was situated on the top of a long ridge running east and west, and just below the road on which I had spent the night the hill fell steeply away to the north in a series of grassy slopes; on these slopes I was told ghooral were plentiful, and several men volunteered to show me over the ground. I was careful not to show my pleasure at this offer and, selecting three men, I set out, telling the Headman that if I found the ghooral as plentiful as he said they were, I would shoot two for the village in addition to shooting one for my men.

Crossing the road, we went down a very steep ridge, keeping a sharp look-out to right and left, but saw nothing. Half a mile down the hill the ravines converged, and from their junction there was a good view of the rocky and grass-covered slope to the right. For some minutes I had been sitting with my back to a solitary pine which grew at this spot, scanning the slope, when a movement high up on the hill caught my eye. When the movement was repeated I saw it was a ghooral flapping its ears; the animal was standing in grass, and only its head was visible. The men had not seen the movement, and as the head was now stationary and blended in with its surroundings it was not possible to point it out to them. Giving them a general idea of the animal's position, I made them sit down and watch while I took a shot. I was armed with an old Martini Henry rifle, a weapon that atoned for its vicious kick by being dead accurate – up to any range. The distance was as near two hundred yards as made no matter and, lying down and resting the rifle on a convenient pine-root, I took careful aim, and fired.

The smoke from the black-powder cartridge obscured my view, and the men said nothing had happened and that I had probably fired at a rock or a bunch of dead leaves. Retaining my position, I reloaded the rifle and presently saw the grass, a little below where I had fired, moving, and the hind quarters of the ghooral appeared. When the whole animal was free of the grass it started to roll over and over, gaining momentum as it came down the steep hill. When it was half-way down it disappeared into heavy grass, and disturbed two ghooral that had been lying up there. Sneezing their alarm call, the two animals dashed out of the grass and went bounding up the hill. The range was shorter now, and, adjusting the leaf sight, 1waited until the bigger of the two slowed down, and put a bullet through its back, and as the other one turned and made off diagonally across the hill, I shot it through the shoulder.

On occasions one is privileged to accomplish the seemingly impossible. Lying in an uncomfortable position and shooting up at an angle of sixty degrees at a range of two hundred yards at the small white mark on the ghooral's throat, there did not appear to be one chance in a million of the shot coming off, and yet the heavy lead bullet driven by black powder had not been deflected by a hair's breadth and had gone true to its mark, killing the animal instantaneously. Again, on the steep hill-side, which was broken up by small ravines and jutting rocks, the dead animal had slipped and rolled straight to the spot where its two companions were lying up; and before it had cleared the patch of grass the two companions in their turn were slipping and rolling down the hill. As the three dead animals landed in the ravine in front of us it was amusing to observe the surprise and delight of the men who never before had seen a rifle in action. All thought of the man-eater was for the time being forgotten as they scrambled down into the ravine to retrieve the bag.

The expedition was a great success in more ways than one; for in addition to providing a ration of meat for everyone, it gained me the confidence of the entire village. Shikar yarns, as everyone knows, never lose anything in repetition, and while the ghooral were being skinned and divided up, the three men who had accompanied me gave full rein to their imagination, and from where I sat in the open, having breakfast, I could hear the exclamations of the assembled crowd when they were told that the ghooral had been shot at a range of over a mile, and that the magic bullets used had not only killed the animals – like that – but had also drawn them to the sahib's feet.

After the midday meal the Headman asked me where I wanted to go, and how many men I wished to take with me. From the eager throng of men who pressed round I selected two of my late companions, and with them to guide me set off to visit the scene of the last human tragedy.

The people of our hills arc Hindus and cremate their dead, and when one of their number has been carried off by a man-eater it is incumbent on the relatives to recover some portion of the body for cremation, even if it be only a few splinters of bone. In the case of this woman the cremation ceremony was yet to be performed, and as we started out, the relatives requested us to bring back any portion of the body we might find.

From early boyhood I have made a hobby of reading and interpreting jungle signs. In the present case I had the account of the eyewitnesses who were present when the woman was killed, but eyewitnesses are not always reliable, whereas jungle signs are a true record of all that has transpired. On arrival at the spot a glance at the ground showed me that the tiger could only have approached the tree one way without being seen, and that was up the ravine. Entering the ravine a hundred yards below the tree, and working up, I found the pug-marks of a tiger in some fine earth that had sifted down between two big rocks; these pug-marks showed the animal to be a tigress, a little past her prime. Farther up the ravine, and some ten yards from the tree, the tigress had lain down behind a rock, presumably to wait for the woman to climb down from the tree. The victim had been the first to cut all the leaves she needed, and as she was letting herself down by a branch some two inches in diameter the tigress had crept forward an<l, standing up on her hind legs, had caught the woman by the foot and pulled her down into the ravine. The branch showed the desperation with which the unfortunate woman had clung to it, for adhering to the rough oak-bark where the branch, and eventually the leaves, had slipped through her grasp were strands of skin which had been torn from the palms of her hands and fingers. Where the tigress had killed the woman there were signs of a struggle and a big patch of dried blood; from here the blood trail, now dry but distinctly visible, led across the ravine and up the opposite bank. Following the blood trail from where it left the ravine, we found the place in the bushes where the tigress had eaten her kill.

It is a popular belief that man-eaters do not eat the head, hands, and feet of their human victims. This is incorrect. Man-eaters, if not disturbed, eat everything – including the blood-soaked clothes, as I found on one occasion; however, that is another story, and will be told some other time.

On the present occasion we found the woman's clothes, and a few pieces of bone which we wrapped up in the clean cloth we had brought for the purpose. Pitifully little as these remains were, they would suffice for the cremation ceremony which would ensure the ashes of the high-caste woman reaching Mother Ganges.

After tea I visited the scene of yet another tragedy. Separated from the main village by the public road was a small holding of a few acres. The owner of this holding had built himself a hut on the hill-side just above the road. The man's wife and the mother of his two children, a boy and a girl aged four and six respectively, was the younger of two sisters. These two sisters were out cutting grass one day on the hill above the hut when the tigress suddenly appeared and carried off the elder sister. For a hundred yards the younger woman ran after the tigress brandishing her sickle and screaming at the tigress to let her sister go and take her instead. This incredible act of heroism was witnessed by the people in the main village. After carrying the dead woman for a hundred yards the tigress put her down and turned on her pursuer. With a loud roar it sprang at the brave woman, who, turning, raced down the hill-side, across the road, and into the village, evidently with the intention of telling the people what they, unknown to her, had already witnessed. The woman's incoherent noises were at the time attributed to loss of breath, fear, and excitement, and it was not until the rescue party that had set out with all speed had returned, unsuccessful, that it was found the woman had lost her power of speech. I was told this tale in the village, and when I climbed the path to the two-roomed hut where the woman was engaged in washing clothes, she had then been dumb a twelve-month.

Except for a strained look in her eyes, the dumb woman appeared to be quite normal and, when I stopped to speak to her and tell her I had come to try and shoot the tiger that had killed her sister, she put her hands together and stooping down touched my feet, making me feel a wretched impostor. True, I had come with the avowed object of shooting the man-eater, but with an animal that had the reputation of never killing twice in the same locality, never returning to a kill, and whose domain extended over an area of many hundred square miles, the chance of my accomplishing my object was about as good as finding a needle in two haystacks.

Plans in plenty I had made, way back in Naini Tal; one I had already tried, and wild horses would not induce me to try it again, and the others – now that I was on the ground – were just as unattractive. Further, there was no one I could ask for advice, for this was the first man-eater that had ever been known in Kumaon; and yet something would have to be done. So for the next three days I wandered through the jungles from sunrise to sun-set, visiting all the places for miles round where the villagers told me there was a chance of my seeing the tigress.

I would like to interrupt my tale here for a few minutes to refute a rumour current throughout the hills, that on this, and on several subsequent occasions, I assumed the dress of a hill woman and, going into the jungle, attracted the man-eaters to myself and killed them with either a sickle or an axe. All I have ever done in the matter of alteration of dress has been to borrow a sari and with it draped round me cut grass, or climbed into trees and cut leaves, and in no case

Jim Corbett

has the ruse proved successful; though on two occasions – to my knowledge – man-eaters have stalked the tree I was on, taking cover, on one occasion behind a rock and on the other behind a fallen tree, and giving me no opportunity of shooting them.

To continue. As the tigress now appeared to have left this locality, I decided, much to the regret of the people of Pali, to move to Champawat, fifteen miles due east of Pali. Making an early start, I breakfasted at Dhunaghat, and completed the journey to Champawat by sunset. The roads in this area were considered very unsafe, and men only moved from village to village or to the bazaars in large parties. After leaving Dhunaghat, my party of eight was added to by men from villages adjoining the road, and we arrived at Champawat thirty strong. Some of the men who joined me had been in a party of twenty men who had visited Champawat two months earlier, and they told me the following very pitiful story.

'The road for a few miles on this side of Champawat runs along the south face of the hill, parallel to and about fifty yards above the valley. Two months ago a party of twenty of us men were on our way to the bazaar at Champawat, and as we were going along this length of the road at about midday, we were startled by hearing the agonized cries of a human being coming from the valley below. Huddled together on the edge of the road, we cowered in fright as these cries drew nearer and nearer, and presently into view came a tiger, carrying a naked woman. The woman's hair was trailing on the ground on one side of the tiger, and her feet on the other – the tiger was holding her by the small of the back – and she was beating her chest and calling alternately on God and man to help her. Fifty yards from, and in clear view of us, the tiger passed with its burden, and when the cries had died away in the distance we continued on our way.'

'And you twenty men did nothing?'

'No, sahib, we did nothing, for we were afraid, and what can men do when they are afraid? And further, even if we had been able to rescue the woman without angering the tiger and bringing misfortune on ourselves, it would have availed the woman nothing, for she was covered with blood and would of a surety have died of her wounds.'

I subsequently learned that the victim belonged to a village near Champawat, and that she had been carried off by the tiger while collecting dry sticks. Her companions had run back to the village and raised an alarm, and just as a rescue party was starting, the twenty frightened mm arrived. As these men knew the direction in which the tiger had gone with its victim, they joined the party, and can best carry on the story.

'We were fifty or sixty strong when we set out to rescue the woman, and several of the party were armed with guns. A furlong from where the sticks collected by the woman were lying, and from where she had been carried off, we found her torn clothes. Thereafter the men started beating their drums and firing off their guns, and in this way we proceeded for more than a mile right up to the head of the valley, where we found the woman, who was little more than a girl, lying dead on a great slab of rock. Beyond licking off all the blood and making her body clean the tiger had not touched her, and, there being no woman in our party, we men averted our faces as we wrapped her body in the loincloths which one and another gave, for she looked as she lay on her back as one who sleeps, and would waken in shame when touched.'

With experiences such as these to tell and re-tell through the long night watches behind fast-shut doors, it is little wonder that the character and outlook on life of people living year after year in a man-eater country should change, and that one coming from the outside should feel that he had stepped right into a world of stark realities and the rule of the tooth and claw, which forced man in the reign of the sabre-toothed tiger to shelter in dark caverns. I was young and inexperienced in those far-off Champawat days, but, even so, the conviction I came to after a brief sojourn in that stricken land, that there is no more terrible thing than to live and have one's being under the shadow of a man-eater, has been strengthened by thirty-two years' subsequent experience.

The Tahsildar of Champawat, to whom I had been given letters of introduction, paid me a visit that night at the Dak Bungalow, where I was putting up, and suggested I should move next day to a bungalow a few miles away, in the vicinity of which many human beings had been killed

Early next morning, accompanied by the Tahsildar, I set out for the bungalow, and while I was having breakfast on the veranda two men arrived with news that a cow had been killed by a tiger in a village ten miles away. The Tahsildar excused himself to attend to some urgent work at Champawat, and said he would return to the bungalow in the evening and stay the night with me. My guides were good walkers, and as the track went down hill most of the way we covered the ten miles in record time. Arrived at the village I was taken to a cattle-shed in which I found a week-old calf, killed and partly eaten by a leopard. Not having the time or the inclination to shoot the leopard, I rewarded my guides and retraced my steps to the bungalow. Here I found the Tahsildar had not returned, and as there was still an hour or more of daylight left I went out with the chowkidar of the bungalow to look at a place where he informed me a tiger was in the habit of drinking; this place I found to be the head of the spring which supplied the garden with irrigation water. In the soft earth round the spring were tiger pug-marks several days old, but these tracks were quite different from the pug-marks I had seen, and carefully examined, in the ravine in which the woman of Pali village had been killed.

On returning to the bungalow I found the Tahsildar was back, and as we sat on the veranda I told him of my day's experience. Expressing regret at my having had to go so far on a wild-goose chase, he rose, saying that as he had a long way to go he must start at once. This announcement caused me no little surprise, for twice that day he had said he would stay the night with me. It was not the question of his staying the night that concerned me, but the risk he was taking; however, he was deaf to all my arguments and, as he stepped off the veranda into the dark night, with only one man following hint carrying a smoky lantern which gave a mere glimmer of light, to do a walk of four miles in a locality in which men only moved in large parties in daylight, I took off my hat to a very brave man. Having watched him out of sight, I turned and entered the bungalow.

I have a tale to tell of that bungalow, but I will not tell it here, for this is a book of jungle stories, and tales 'beyond the laws of nature' do not consort well with such stories.

II

I spent the following morning in going round the very extensive fruit orchard and tea-garden and in having a bath at the spring, and at about midday the Tahsildar, much to my relief, returned safely from Champawat.

I was standing talking to him while looking down a long sloping hill with a village surrounded by cultivated land in the distance, when I saw a man leave the village and start up the hill in our direction. As the man drew nearer I saw he was alternately running and walking, and was quite evidently the bearer of important news. Telling the Tahsildar I would return in a few minutes, I set off at a run down the hill, and when the man saw me coming he sat down to take breath. As soon as I was near enough to hear him he called out, 'Come quickly, sahib, the man-eater has just killed a girl.' 'Sit still,' I called back, and turning ran up to the bungalow. I passed the news on to the Tahsildar while I was getting a rifle and some cartridges, and asked him to follow me down to the village.

The man who had come for me was one of those exasperating individuals whose legs and tongue cannot function at the same time. When he opened his mouth he stopped dead, and when he started to run his mouth closed; so telling him to shut his mouth and lead the way, we ran in silence down the hill.

At the village an excited crowd of men, women, and children awaited us and, as usually happens on these occasions, all started to talk at the same time. One man was vainly trying to quieten the babel. I led him aside and asked him to tell me what had happened. Pointing to some scattered oak-trees on a gentle slope a furlong or so from the village, he said a dozen people were collecting dry sticks under the trees when a tiger suddenly appeared and caught one of their number, a girl sixteen or seventeen years of age. The rest of the party had run back to the village, and as it was known that I was staying at the bungalow, a man had immediately been dispatched to inform me.

The wife of the man I was speaking to had been of the party, and she now pointed out the tree, on the shoulder of the hill, under which the girl had been taken. None of the party had looked back to see if the tiger was carrying away its victim and, if so, in which direction it had gone.

Instructing the crowd not to make a noise, and to remain in the village until I returned, I set off in the direction of the tree. The ground here was quite open, and it was difficult to conceive how an animal the size of a tiger could have approached twelve people unseen, and its presence not detected, until attention had been attracted by the choking sound made by the girl.

The spot where the girl had been killed was marked by a pool of blood, and near it, and in vivid contrast to the crimson pool, was a broken necklace of brightly coloured blue beads which the girl had been wearing. From this spot the track led up and round the shoulder of the hill.

The track of the tigress was clearly visible. On one side of it were great splashes of blood where the girl's head had hung down, and on the other side the trail df her feet. Half a mile up the hill I found the girl's sari, and on the brow of the hill her skirt. Once again the tigress was carrying a naked woman, but mercifully on this occasion her burden was dad.

On the brow of the hill the track led through a thicket of blackthorn, on the thorns of which long strands of the girl's raven-black hair had caught. Beyond this was a bed of nettles through which the tigress had gone, and I was looking for a way round this obstruction when I heard footsteps behind me. Turning round, I saw a man armed with a rifle coming towards me. I asked him why he had followed me when I had left instructions at the village that no one was to leave it. He said the Tahsildar had instructed him to accompany me, and that he was afraid to disobey orders. As he appeared determined to carry out his orders, and to argue the point would have meant the loss of valuable time, I told him to remove the heavy pair of boots he was wearing and, when he had hidden them under a bush, I advised him to keep close to me, and to keep a sharp look-out behind.

I was wearing a very thin pair of stockings, shorts, and a pair of rubber-soled shoes, and as there appeared to be no way round the nettles I followed the tigress through them – much to my discomfort.

Beyond the nettles the blood trail turned sharply to the left, and went straight down the very steep hill, which was densely clothed with bracken and ringals. A hundred yards down, the blood trail led into a narrow and very steep watercourse, down which the tigress had gone with some difficulty, as could be seen from the dislodged stones and earth. I followed this watercourse for five or six hundred yards, my companion getting more and more agitated the farther we went. A dozen times he caught my arm and whispered – in a voice full of tears – that he could hear the tiger, either on one side or the other, or behind us. Half-way down the hill we came on a great pinnacle of rock some thirty feet high, and as the man had by now had all the man-eater hunting he could stand, I told him to climb the rock and remain on it until I returned. Very gladly he went up, and when he straddled the top and signalled to me that he was all right I continued on down the watercourse, which, after skirting round the rock, went straight down for a hundred yards to where it met a deep ravine coming down from the left. At the junction was a small pool, and as I approached it I saw patches of blood on my side of the water.

The tigress had carried the girl straight down to this spot, and my approach had disturbed her at her meal. Splinters of bone were scattered round the deep pug-marks into which discoloured water was slowly seeping, and at the edge of the pool was an object which had puzzled me as I came down the watercourse, and which I now found was part of a human leg. In all the subsequent years I have hunted man-eaters I have not seen anything as pitiful as that young, comely leg – bitten off a little below the knee as clean as though severed by the stroke of an axe – out of which the warm blood was trickling.

While looking at the leg I had forgotten all about the tigress until I suddenly felt that I was in great danger. Hurriedly grounding the butt of the rifle I put two fingers on the triggers, raising my head as I did so, and saw a little earth, from the fifteen-foot bank in front of me, come rolling down the steep side and plop into the pool. I was new to this game of man-eater hunting, or I should not have exposed myself to an attack in the way I had done. My prompt action in pointing the rifle upwards had possibly saved my life, and in stopping her spring, or in turning to get away, the tigress had dislodged the earth from the top of the bank.

The bank was too steep for scrambling, and the only

way of getting up was to take it at a run. Going up the water-course a short distance I sprinted down, took the pool in my stride, and got far enough up the other side to grasp a bush and pull myself on to the bank. A bed of Strobilanthes, the bent stalks of which were slowly regaining their upright position, showed where, and how recently, the tigress had passed, and a little farther on under an overhanging rock I found where she had left her kill when she came to have a look at me.

Her tracks now – as she carried away the girl – led into a wilderness of rocks, some acres in extent, where the going was both difficult and dangerous. The cracks and chasms between the rocks were masked with ferns and blackberry vines, and a false step, which might easily have resulted in a broken limb, would have been fatal. Progress under these conditions was of necessity slow, and the tigress was taking advantage of it to continue her meal. A dozen times I found where she had rested, and after each of these rests the blood trail became more distinct.

This was her four hundred and thirty-sixth human kill, and she was quite accustomed to being disturbed at her meals by rescue parties, but this, I think, was the first time she had been followed up so persistently, and she now began to show her resentment by growling. To appreciate a tiger's growl to the full it is necessary to be situated as I then was – rocks all round with dense vegetation between, and the imperative necessity of testing each footstep to avoid falling headlong into unseen chasms and caves.

I cannot expect you who read this at your fireside to appreciate my feelings at the time. The sound of the growling and the expectation of an attack terrified me at the same time as it gave me hope. If the ogress lost her temper sufficiently to launch an attack, it would not only give me an opportunity of accomplishing the object for which I had come, but it would enable me to get even with her for all the pain and suffering she had caused.

The growling, however, was only a gesture, and, when she found that instead of shooing me off it was bringing me faster on her heels, she abandoned it.

I had now been on her track for over four hours. Though I had repeatedly seen the undergrowth moving, I had not seen so much as a hair of her hide, and a glance at the shadows climbing up the opposite hill-side warned me it was time to retrace my steps if I was to reach the village before dark.

The late owner of the severed leg was a Hindu, and some portion of her would be needed for the cremation, so as I passed the pool I dug a hole in the bank and buried the leg where it would be safe from the tigress, and could be found when wanted.

My companion on the rock was very relieved to see me. My long absence, and the growling he had heard, had convinced him that the tigress had secured another kill, and his difficulty, as he quite frankly admitted, was how he was going to get back to the village alone.

I thought when we were climbing down the watercourse that I knew of no more dangerous proceeding than walking in front of a nervous man carrying a loaded gun, but I changed my opinion when on walking behind him he slipped and fell, and I saw where the muzzle of his gun – a converted .450 without a safety catch – was pointing. Since that day – except when accompanied by Ibbotson – I have made it a hard-and-fast rule to go alone when hunting man-eaters, for if one's companion is unarmed it is difficult to protect him, and if he is armed, it is even more difficult to protect oneself.

Arrived at the crest of the hill, where the man had hidden his boots, I sat down to have a smoke and think out my plans for the morrow.

The tigress would finish what was left of the kill during the night, and would to a certainty lie up among the rocks next day.

On the ground she was on there was very little hope of my being able to stalk her, and if I disturbed her without getting a shot, she would probably leave the locality and I should lose touch with her. A beat therefore was the only thing to do, provided I could raise sufficient men.

I was sitting on the south edge of a great amphitheatre of hills, without a habitation of any kind in sight. A stream entering from the west had fretted its way down, cutting a deep valley right across the amphitheatre. To the east the stream had struck solid rock, and turning north had left the amphitheatre by a narrow gorge.

The hill in front of me, rising to a height of some two thousand feet, was clothed in short grass with a pine-tree dotted here and there, and the hill to the east was too precipitous for anything but a ghooral to negotiate. If I could collect sufficient men to man the entire length of the ridge from the stream to the precipitous hill, and get them to stir up the tigress, her most natural line of retreat would be through the narrow gorge.

Admittedly a very difficult beat, for the steep hill-side facing north, on which I had left the tigress, was densely wooded and roughly three-quarters of a mile long and half a mile wide; however, if I could get the beaters to carry out instructions, there was a reasonable chance of my getting a shot.

The Tashildar was waiting for me at the village. I explained the position to him, and asked him to take immediate steps to collect as many men as he could, and to meet me at ten o'clock the following morning at the tree where the girl had been killed. Promising to do his best, he left for Champawat, while I climbed the hill to the bungalow.

I was up at crack of dawn next morning, and after a substantial meal told my men to pack up and wait for me at Champawat, and went down to have another look at the ground I intended beating. I could find nothing wrong with the plans I had made, and an hour before my time I was at the spot where I had asked the Tahsildar to meet me.

That he would have a hard time in collecting the men I had no doubt, for the fear of the man-eater had sunk deep into the countryside, and more than mild persuasion would be needed to make the men leave the shelter of their homes. At ten o'clock the Tashildar and one man turned up, and thereafter the men came in twos, and threes, and tens, until by midday two hundred and ninety-eight had collected.

The Tahsildar had let it be known that he would turn a blind eye towards all unlicensed fire-arms, and further that he would provide ammunition where required; and the weapons that were produced that day would have stocked a museum.

When the men were assembled and had received the ammunition they needed I took them to the brow of the hill where the girl's skirt was lying, and pointing to a pine-tree on the opposite hill that had been struck by lightning and stripped of bark, I told them to line themselves up along the ridge and, when they saw me wave a handkerchief from under the pine, those of them who were armed were to fire off their pieces, while the others beat drums, shouted, and rolled down rocks, and that no one was on any account to leave the ridge until I returned and personally collected him. When I was assured that all present had heard and understood my instructions, I set off with the Tahsildar, who said he would be safer with me than with the beaters, whose guns would probably burst and cause many casualties.

Making a wide detour, I crossed the upper end of the valley, gained the opposite hill, and made my way down to the blasted pine. From here the hill went steeply down, and the Tahsildar, who had on a thin pair of patent-leather shoes, said it was impossible for him to go any farther. While he was removing his inadequate footgear to ease his blisters, the men on the ridge, thinking I had forgotten to give the pre-arranged signal, fired off their guns and set up a great shout. I was still a hundred and fifty yards from the gorge, and that I did not break my neck a dozen times in covering this distance was due to my having been brought up on the hills, and being in consequence as sure-footed as a goat.

As I ran down the hill I noticed that there was a patch of green grass near the mouth of the gorge, and as there was no time to look round for a better place, I sat down in the grass, with my back to the hill down which I had just come. The grass was about two feet high and hid half my body, and if I kept perfectly still there was a good chance of my not being seen. Facing me was the hill that was being beaten, and the gorge that I hoped the tigress would make for was behind my left shoulder.

Pandemonium had broken loose on the ridge. Added to the fusillade of guns was the wild beating of drums and the shouting of hundreds of men, and when the din was at its worst I caught sight of the tigress bounding down a grassy slope between two ravines to my right front, and about three hundred yards away. She had only gone a short distance when the Tahsildar from his position under the pine let off both barrels of his shot-gun. On hearing the shots the tigress whipped round and went straight back the way she had come, and as she disappeared into thick cover I threw up my rifle and sent a despairing bullet after her.

The men on the ridge, hearing the three shots, not unnaturally concluded that the tigress had been killed. They emptied all their guns and gave a final yell, and I was holding my breath and listening for the screams that would herald the tigress's arrival on the ridge, when she suddenly broke cover to my left front and, taking the stream at a bound, came straight for the gorge. The .500 modified cordite rifle, sighted at sea-level, shot high at this altitude, and when the tigress stopped dead I thought the bullet had gone over her back, and that she had pulled up on finding her retreat cut off; as a matter of fact I had hit her all right, but a little far back. Lowering her head, she half-turned towards me, giving me a beautiful shot at the point of her shoulder at a range of less than thirty yards. She flinched at this second shot but continued, with her ears laid flat and bared teeth, to stand her ground, while I sat with rifle to shoulder trying to think what it would be best for me to do when she charged, for the rifle was empty and I had no more cartridges. Three cartridges were all that I had brought with me, for I never thought I should get a chance of firing more than two shots, and the third cartridge was for – an emergency.

Fortunately the wounded animal most unaccountably decided against a charge. Very slowly she turned, crossed the stream to her right, climbed over some fallen rocks, and found a narrow ledge that went diagonally up and across the face of the precipitous hill to where there was a great flat projecting rock. Where this rock joined the cliff small bush had found root-hold, and going up to it the tigress started to strip its branches. Throwing caution to the winds I shouted to the Tahsildar to bring me his gun. A long reply was shouted back, the only word of which I caught was 'feet'. Laying down my rifle I took the hill at a run, grabbed the gun out of the Tahsildar's hands and raced back.

As I approached the stream the tigress left the bush and came out on the projecting rock towards me. When I was within twenty feet of her I raised the gun and found to my horror that there was a gap of about three-eighths of an inch between the barrels and the breech-lock. The gun had not burst when both barrels had been fired, and would probably not burst now, but there was danger of being blinded by a blow back. However, the risk would have to be taken, and, aligning the great blob of a bead that did duty as a sight on the tigress's open mouth, I fired. Maybe I bobbed, or maybe the gun was not capable of throwing the cylindrical bullet accurately for twenty feet; anyway, the missile missed the tigress's mouth and struck her on the right paw, from where I removed it later with my finger-nails. Fortunately she was at her last gasp, and the tap on the foot was sufficient to make her lurch forward. She came to rest with her head projecting over the side of the rock.

From the moment the tigress had broken cover in her attempt to get through the gorge I had forgotten the beaters, until I was suddenly reminded of their existence by hearing a shout, from a short distance up the hill, of 'There it is on the rock! Pull it down and let us hack it to bits.' I could not believe my ears when I heard 'hack it to bits', and yet I had heard aright, for others now had caught sight of the tigress, and from all over the hill-side the shout was being repeated.

The ledge by which the wounded animal had gained the projecting rock was fortunately on the opposite side from the beaters, and was just wide enough to permit my shuffling along it sideways. As I reached the rock and stepped over the tigress – hoping devoutly she was dead, for I had not had time to carry out the usual test of pelting her with stones – the men emerged from the forest and came running across the open, brandishing guns, axes, rusty swords, and spears.

At the rock, which was twelve to fourteen feet in height, their advance was checked, for the outer face had been worn smooth by the stream when in spate and afforded no foothold even for their bare toes. The rage of the crowd on seeing their dread enemy was quite understandable, for there was not a man among them who had not suffered at her hands. One man, who appeared demented and was acting as ring-leader, was shouting over and over again as he ran to and fro brandishing a sword, 'This is the shaitan that killed my wife and my two sons.' As happens with crowds, the excitement died down as suddenly as it had flared up, and to the credit of the man who had lost his wife and sons be it said that he was the first to lay down his weapon. He came near to the rock and said, 'We were mad, sahib, when we saw our enemy, but the madness has now passed, and we ask you and the Tahsildar sahib to forgive us.' Extracting the unspent cartridge, I laid the gun across the tigress and hung down by my hands and was assisted to the ground. When I showed the men how I had gained the rock the dead animal was very gently lowered and carried to an open spot, where all could crowd round and look at her.

When the tigress had stood on the rock looking down at

me I had noticed that there was something wrong with her mouth, and on examining her now I found that the upper and lower canine teeth on the right side of her mouth were broken, the upper one in half, and the lower one right down to the bone. This permanent injury to her teeth – the result of a gun-shot wound – had prevented her from killing her natural prey, and had been the cause of her becoming a man-eater.

The men begged me not to skin the tigress there, and asked me to let them have her until nightfall to carry through their villages, saying that if their womenfolk and children did not see her with their own eyes, they would not believe that their dread enemy was dead.

Two saplings were now cut and laid one on either side of the tigress, and with pugrees, waistbands, and loin-cloths she was carefully and very securely lashed to them. When all was ready the saplings were manned and we moved to the foot of the precipitous hill; the men preferred to take the tigress up this hill, on the far side of which their villages lay, to going up the densely wooded hill which they had just beaten. Two human ropes were made by the simple expedient of the man behind taking a firm grip of the waistband, or other portion of clothing, of the man in front of him. When it was considered that the ropes were long and strong enough to stand the strain, they attached themselves to the saplings, and with men on either side to hold the feet of the bearers and give them foot-hold, the procession moved up the hill, looking for all the world like an army of ants carrying a beetle up the face of a wall. Behind the main army was a second and a smaller one – the Tahsildar being carried up. Had the ropes broken at any stage of that thousand-foot climb, the casualties would have been appalling, but the rope did not break. The men gained the crest of the hill and set off eastwards, singing on their triumphal march, while the Tahsildar and I turned west and made for Champawat.

Our way lay along the ridge, and once again I stood among the blackthorn bushes, on the thorns of which long tresses of the girl's hair had caught, and for the last time looked down into the amphitheatre which had been the scene of our recent exploit.

On the way down the hill the beaters had found the head of the unfortunate girl, and a thin column of smoke rising straight up into the still air from the mouth of the gorge showed where the relations were performing the last rites of the Champawat man-eater's last victim, on the very spot on which the man-eater had been shot.

After dinner, while I was standing in the courtyard of the Tahsil, I saw a long procession of pine-torches winding its way down the opposite hill-side, and presently the chanting of a hill song by a great concourse of men was borne up on the still night air. An hour later, the tigress was laid down at my feet.

It was difficult to skin the animal with so many people crowding round, and to curtail the job I cut the head and paws from the trunk and left them adhering to the skin, to be dealt with later. A police guard was then mounted over the carcass, and next day, when all the people of the countryside were assembled, the trunk, legs, and tail of the tigress were cut up into small pieces and distributed. These pieces of flesh and bone were required for the lockets which hill children wear round their necks, and the addition of a piece of tiger to the other potent charms is credited with giving the wearer courage, as well as immunity from the attacks of wild animals. The fingers of the girl, which the tigress had swallowed whole, were sent to me in spirits by the Tahsildar, and were buried by me in the Naini Tal lake close to the Nandadevi temples.

While I had been skinning the tigress the Tahsildar and his staff, assisted by the Headman and greybeards of the surrounding villages and merchants of the Champawat bazaar, had been busy drawing up a programme for a great feast and dance for the morrow, at which I was to preside. Round about midnight, when the last of the great throng of men had left with shouts of delight at being able to use roads and village paths that the man-eater had closed for four years, I had a final smoke with the Tahsildar, and telling him that I could not stay any longer and that he would have to take my place at the festivities, my men and I set off on our seventy-five-mile journey, with two days in hand to do it in.

At sunrise I left my men and, with the tigress's skin strapped to the saddle of my horse, rode on ahead to put in a few hours in cleaning the skin at Dabidhura, where I intended spending the night. When passing the hut on the hill at Pali it occurred to me that it would be some little satisfaction to the dumb woman to know that her sister had been avenged, so leaving the horse to browse – he had been bred near the snow-line and could eat anything from oak-trees to nettles – I climbed the hill to the hut, and spread out the skin with the head supported on a stone facing the door. The children of the house had been round-eyed spectators of these proceedings and, hearing me talking to them, their mother, who was inside rooking, came to the door.

I am not going to hazard any theories about shock, and counter-shock, for I know nothing of these matters. All I know is that this woman, who was alleged to have been dumb a twelve-month and who four days previously had made no attempt to answer my questions, was now running backwards and forwards from the hut to the road calling to her husband and the people in the village to come quickly and see what the sahib had brought. This sudden return of speech appeared greatly to mystify the children, who could not take their eyes off their mother's face.

I rested in the village while a dish of tea was being prepared for me and told the people who thronged round how the man-eater had been killed. An hour later I continued my journey, and for half a mile along my way I could hear the shouts of goodwill of the men of Pali.

I had a very thrilling encounter with a leopard the following morning, which I only mention because it delayed my start from Dabidhura and put an extra strain on my small mount and myself. Fortunately the little pony was as strong on his legs as he was tough inside, and by holding his tail on the up-grades, riding him on the flat, and running behind him on the down-grades, we covered the forty-five miles to Naini Tal between g a.m. and 6 p.m.

At a durbar held in Naini Tal a few months later Sir John Hewett, Lieutenant-Governor of the United Provinces, presented the Tahsildar of Champawat with a gun, and the man who accompanied me when I was looking for the girl, with a beautiful hunting-knife, for the help they had given me. Both weapons were suitably engraved, and will be handed down as heirlooms in the respective families.

ROBIN

I never saw either of his parents. The Knight of the Broom I purchased him from said he was a spaniel, that his name was Pincha, and that his father was a 'Keen gun dog'. This is all 1 can tell you about his pedigree.

I did not want a pup, and it was quite by accident that I happened to be with a friend when the litter of seven was decanted from a very filthy basket for her inspection. Pincha was the smallest and the thinnest of the litter, and it was quite evident he had reached the last ditch in his fight for survival. Leaving his little less miserable brothers and sisters, he walked once round me, and then curled himself up between my big feet. When I picked him up and put him inside my coat – it was a bitterly cold morning – he tried to show his gratitude by licking my face, and I tried to show him I was not aware of his appalling stench.

He was rising three mouths then, and I bought him for fifteen rupees. He is rising thirteen years now, and all the gold in India would not buy him.

When 1 got him home, and he had made his first acquaintance with a square meal, warm water, and soap, we scrapped his kennel name of Pincha and re-christened him Robin, in memory of a faithful old collie who had saved my young brother, aged four, and myself, aged six, from the attack of an infuriated she-bear.

Robin responded to regular meals as parched land does to rain, and after he had been with us for a few weeks, acting on the principle that a boy's and a pup's training cannot be started too early, I took him out one morning, intending to get a little away from him and fire a shot or two to get him used to the sound of gun-fire.

At the lower end of our estate there are some dense thorn bushes, and while I was skirting round them a pea-fowl got up, and forgetting all about Robin, who was following at heel, I brought the bird fluttering down. It landed in the thorn-bushes, and Robin dashed in after it. The bushes were too thick and thorny for me to enter them, so I ran round to the far side, where beyond the bushes was open ground, and beyond that again heavy tree and grass jungle which I knew the wounded bird would make for. The open ground was flooded with morning sunlight, and if I had been armed with a movie camera I should have had an opportunity of securing a unique picture. The pea-fowl, an old hen, with neck-feathers stuck out at right angles, and one wing broken, was making for the tree jungle, while Robin, with stern to the ground, was hanging on to her tail and being dragged along. Running forward, I very foolishly caught the bird by the neck and lifted it clear of the ground, whereon it promptly lashed out with both legs, and sent Robin heels-over-head. In a second he was up and on his feet again, and when I laid the dead bird down, he danced round it, making little dabs alternately at its head and tail. The lesson was over for that morning, and as we returned home it would have been difficult to say which of us was the more proud – Robin, at bringing home his first bird, or I, at having picked a winner out of a filthy basket. The shooting season was now drawing to a close, and for the next few days Robin was not given anything larger than quail, doves, and an occasional partridge to retrieve.

We spent the summer in the hills, and on our annual migration to the foot-hills in November, at the end of a long fifteen-mile march as we turned a sharp corner, one of a big troop of langurs jumped off the hill-side and crossed the road a few inches in front of Robin's nose. Disregarding my whistle, Robin dashed down the khudside after the langur, which promptly sought safety in a tree. The ground was open with a few trees here and there, and after going steeply down for thirty or forty yards flattened out for a few yards, before going sharply down into the valley below. On the right-hand side of this flat ground there were a few bushes, with a deep channel scoured out by rain-water running through them. Robin had hardly entered these bushes when he was out again, and with ears laid back and tail tucked in was running for dear life, with an enormous leopard bounding after him and gaining on him at every bound. I was unarmed, and all the assistance I could render was to 'Ho' and 'Har' at the full extent of my lungs. The men carrying M.'s dandy joined in lustily, the pandemonium reaching its climax when the hundred or more langurs added their alarm-calls, in varying keys. For twenty-five or thirty yards the desperate and unequal race continued, and just as the leopard was within reach of Robin, it unaccountably swerved and disappeared into the valley, while Robin circled round a shoulder of the hill and rejoined us on the road. Two very useful lessons Robin learned from his hairbreadth escape, which he never in after-life forgot. First, that it was dangerous to chase langurs, and second that the alarm-call of a langur denoted the presence of a leopard.

In spring, Robin resumed his training where it had been interrupted, but it soon became apparent that his early neglect and starvation had affected his heart, for he fainted now after the least exertion.

There is nothing more disappointing for a gun-dog than to be left at home when his master goes out, and as bird-shooting was now taboo for Robin, I started taking him with me when I went out after big game. He took to this new form of sport as readily as a duck takes to water, and from then on has accompanied me whenever I have been out with a rifle.

The method we employ is to go out early in the morning, pick up the tracks of a leopard or tiger, and follow them. When the pug-marks can be seen, I do the tracking, and when the animal we are after takes to the jungle, Robin does the tracking. In this way we have on occasions followed an animal for miles before coming up with it.

When shooting on foot, it is very much easier to kill an animal outright than when shooting down on it from a machan, or from the back of an elephant. For one thing, when wounded animals have to be followed up on foot, chance shots are not indulged in, and for another, the vital parts are more accessible when shooting on the same level as the animal than when shooting down on it. However, even after exercising the greatest care over the shot, I have sometimes only wounded leopards and tigers, who have rampaged round before being quietened by a second or third shot, and only once during all the years that we have shot together has Robin left me in a tight corner. When he rejoined me after his brief absence that day, we decided that the incident was closed and would never be referred to again, but we are older now and possibly less sensitive, anyway Robin – who has exceeded the canine equivalent of three-score-years-and-ten, and who lies at my feet as I write, on a bed he will never again leave – has with a smile from his wise brown eyes and a wag of his small stump of a tail given me permission to go ahead and tell you the story.

We did not see the leopard until it stepped clear of the thick undergrowth and, coming to a stand, looked back over its left shoulder.

He was an outsized male with a beautiful dark glossy coat, the rosettes on his skin standing out like clear-cut designs on a rich velvet ground. I had an unhurried shot with an accurate rifle at his right shoulder, at the short range of fifteen yards. By how little I missed his heart makes no matter, and while the bullet was kicking up the dust fifty yards away he was high in the air, and, turning a somersault, landed in the thick undergrowth he had a minute before left. For twenty, forty, fifty yards we heard him crashing through the cover, and then the sound ceased as abruptly as it had begun. This sudden cessation of sound could be accounted for in two ways: either the leopard had collapsed and died in his tracks or fifty yards away he had reached 0pen ground.

We had walked far that day; the sun was near setting and we were still four miles from home. This part of the jungle was not frequented by man, and there was not one chance in a million of anyone passing that way by night, and last, and the best reason of all for leaving the leopard, M. was unarmed and could neither be left alone nor taken along to follow up the wounded animal – so we turned to the north and made for home. There was no need for me to mark the spot, for I had walked through these jungles by day – and often by night – for near on half a century, and could have found my way blindfold to any part of them.

Night had only just given place to day the following morning when Robin – who had not been with us the previous evening – and I arrived at the spot I had fired from. Very warily Robin, who was leading, examined the ground where the leopard had stood, and then raising his head and snuffing the air he advanced to the edge of the undergrowth, where the leopard in falling had left great splashes of blood. There was no need for me to examine the blood to determine the position of the wound, for at the short range I had fired at I had seen the bullet strike, and the spurt of dust on the far side was proof that the bullet had gone right through the leopard's body.

It might be necessary later on to follow up the blood trail, but just at present a little rest after our four-mile walk in the dark would do no harm, and might on the other hand prove of great value to us. The sun was near rising, and at that early hour of the morning all the jungle folk were on the move, and it would be advisable to hear what they had to say on the subject of the wounded animal before going farther.

Under a nearby tree I found a dry spot to which the saturating dew had not penetrated, and with Robin stretched out at my feet had finished my cigarette when a chital hind, and then a second and a third, started calling some sixty yards to our left front. Robin sat up and, slowly turning his head, looked at me, and, on catching my eye, as slowly turned back in the direction of the calling deer. He had travelled far along the road of experience since that day he had first heard the alarm-call of a langur, and he knew now – as did every bird and animal within hearing – that the chital were warning the jungle folk of the presence of a leopard.

From the manner in which the chital were calling it was evident that the leopard was in full view of them. A little more patience and they would tell us if he was alive. They had been calling for about five minutes when suddenly, and all together, they called once and again, and then settled down to their regular call; the leopard was alive and had moved, and was now quiet again. All that we needed to know now was the position of the leopard, and this information we could get by stalking the chital.

Moving down-wind for fifty yards we entered the thick undergrowth, and started to stalk the deer – not a difficult task, for Robin can move through any jungle as silently as a cat, and long practice has taught me where to place my feet. The chital were not visible until we were within a few feet of them. They were standing in the open and looking towards the north in the exact direction, as far as I was able to judge, in which the crashing sound of the evening before had ceased.

Up to this point the chital had been of great help to us; they had told us the leopard was lying out in the open and that it was alive, and they had now given us the direction. It had taken us the best part of an hour to acquire this information, and if the chital now caught sight of us and warned the jungle folk of our presence, they would in one second undo the good they had so far done. I was debating whether it would be better to retrace our steps and work down below the calling deer and try to get a shot from behind them, or move them from our vicinity by giving the call of a leopard, when one of the hinds turned her head and looked straight into my face. Next second, with a cry of 'Ware man', they dashed away at top speed. I had only about five yards to cover to reach the open ground, but quick as I was the leopard was quicker, and I was only in time to see his hind quarters and tail disappearing behind some bushes. The chital had very effectively spoilt my chance of a shot, and the leopard would now have to be located and marked down all over again – this time by Robin.

I stood on the open ground for some minutes, to give the leopard time to settle down and the scent he had left in his passage to blow past us, and then took Robin due west across the track of the wind, which was blowing from the north. We had gone about sixty or seventy yards when Robin, who was leading, stopped and turned to face into the wind. Robin is mute in the jungles, and has a wonderful control over his nerves. There is one nerve, however, running down the back of his hind legs, which he cannot control when he is looking at a leopard, or when the scent of a leopard is warm and strong. This nerve was now twitching, and agitating the long hair on the upper part of his hind legs.

A very violent cyclonic storm had struck this part of the forest the previous summer, uprooting a number of trees; it was towards one of these fallen trees, forty yards from where we were standing, that Robin was now looking. The branches were towards us, and on either side of the trunk there were light bushes and a few scattered tufts of short grass.

At any other time Robin and I would have made straight for our quarry; but on this occasion a little extra caution was advisable. Not only were we dealing with an animal who when wounded knows no fear, but in addition we were dealing with a leopard who had had fifteen hours in which to nurse his grievance against man, and who could in consequence be counted on to have all his fighting instincts thoroughly aroused.

When leaving home that morning I had picked up the .275 rifle I had used the previous evening. A good rifle to carry when miles have to be covered, but not the weapon one would select to deal with a wounded leopard; so instead of a direct approach, I picked a line that would take us fifteen yards from, and parallel to, the fallen tree. Step by step, Robin leading, we moved along this line. and had passed the branches and were opposite the trunk when Robin stopped. Taking the direction from him, I presently saw what had attracted his attention – the tip of the leopard's tail slowly raised, and as slowly lowered – the warning a leopard invariably gives before charging. Pivoting to the right on my heels, I had just got the rifle to my shoulder when the leopard burst through the intervening bushes and sprang at us. My bullet, fired more with the object of deflecting him than with any hope of killing or even hitting him, passed under his belly and went through the fleshy part of his left thigh. The crack of the rifle, more than the wound, had the effect of deflecting the leopard sufficiently to make him pass my right shoulder without touching me, and before I could get in another shot, he disappeared into the bushes beyond.

    Robin had not moved from my feet, and together we now examined the ground the leopard had passed over. Blood we found in plenty, but whether it had come from the old wounds torn open by the leopard's violent exertions, or from my recent shot, it was impossible to say. Anyway it made no difference to Robin, who without a moment's hesitation took up the trail. After going through some very heavy cover we came on knee-high undergrowth, and had proceeded about a couple of hundred yards when I saw the leopard get up in front of us, and before I could get the rifle to bear on him, he disappeared under a lantana bush. This bush with its branches resting on the ground was as big as a cottage tent, and in addition to affording the leopard ideal cover gave him all the advantages for launching his next attack.

Robin and I had come very well out of our morning's adventure, and it would have been foolish now, armed as I was, to pursue the leopard farther, so without more ado we turned about and made for home.

Next morning we were back on the ground. From a very early hour Robin had been agitating to make a start, and, ignoring all the interesting smells the jungle holds in the morning, would have made me do the four miles at a run had that been possible.

I had armed myself with a 450/400, and was in consequence feeling much happier than I had done the previous day. When we were several hundred yards from the lantana bush, I made Robin slow down and advance cautiously, for it is never safe to assume that a wounded animal will be found where it has been left hours previously, as the following regrettable incident shows.

A sportsman of my acquaintance wounded a tiger one afternoon, and followed the blood trail for several miles along a valley. Next morning, accompanied by a number of men, one of whom was carrying his empty rifle and leading the way, he set out intending to take up the tracking where he had left off. His way led over the previous day's blood trail, and while still a mile from the spot where the tiger had been left, the leading man, who incidentally was the local shikari, walked on to the wounded tiger and was killed. The rest of the party escaped, some by climbing trees and others by showing a clean pair of heels.

I had marked the exact position of the lantana bush, and now took Robin along a line that would pass a few yards on the lee side of it. Robin knew all that was worth knowing about this method of locating the position of an animal by cutting across the wind, and we had only gone a short distance, and were still a hundred yards from the bush, when he stopped, turned and faced into the wind, and communicated to me that he could smell the leopard. As on the previous day, he was facing a fallen tree which was lying along the edge of, and parallel to, the thick undergrowth through which we had followed the leopard to the lantana bush after he had charged us. On our side of the tree the ground was open, but on the far side there was a dense growth of waist-high basonta bushes. Having signalled to Robin to carry on along our original line, we went past the lantana bush, in which he showed no interest, to a channel washed out by rain-water. Here, removing my coat, I filled it with as many stones as the stitches would hold, and with this improvised sack slung over my shoulder returned to the open ground near the tree.

Resuming my coat, and holding the rifle ready for instant use, I took up a position fifteen yards from the tree and started throwing the stones, first on to the tree and then into the bushes on the far side of it with the object of making the leopard – assuming he was still alive – charge on to the open ground where I could deal with him. When all my ammunition was exhausted I coughed, clapped my hands, and shouted, and neither during the bombardment nor after it did the leopard move or make any sound to indicate that he was alive.

I should now have been justified in walking straight up to the tree and looking on the far side of it, but remembering an old jungle saying, 'It is never safe to assume that a leopard is dead until it has been skinned', I set out to circle round the tree, intending to reduce the size of the circles until I could see right under the branches and along the whole length of the trunk. I made the radius of the first circle about twenty-five yards, and had gone two-thirds of the way round when Robin stopped. As I looked down to see what had attracted his attention, there were a succession of deep-throated, angry grunts, and the leopard made straight for us. All I could see was the under-growth being violently agitated in a direct line towards us, and I only just had time to swing half-right and bring the rifle up, when the head and shoulders of the leopard appeared out of the bushes a few feet away.

The leopard's spring and my shot were simultaneous, and side-stepping to the left and leaning back as far as I could, I fired the second barrel from my hip into his side as he passed me.

When a wounded animal, be he leopard or tiger, makes a headlong charge and fails to contact he invariably carries on and does not return to the attack until he is again disturbed.

I had side-stepped to the left to avoid crushing Robin, and when I looked down for him now, he was nowhere to be seen. For the first time in all the years we had hunted together we had parted company in a tight corner, and he was now probably trying to find his way home, with very little chance of being able to avoid the many dangers that lay before him in the intervening four miles of jungle. Added to the natural dangers he would have to face in a jungle with which, owing to its remoteness from home, he was not familiar, was the weak condition of his heart. It was therefore with very great misgivings that I turned about to go in search of him, and as I did so, I caught sight of his head projecting from behind a tree-trunk at the edge of a small

clearing a hundred yards away. When I raised my hand and beckoned, he disappeared into the undergrowth, but a little later, with drooped eyes and drooping ears, he crept silently to my feet. Laying down the rifle, I picked him up in my arms and, for the second time in his life, he licked my face – telling me as he did so, with little throaty sounds, how glad he was to find me unhurt, and how terribly ashamed he was of himself for having parted company from me.

Our reactions to the sudden and quite unexpected danger that had confronted us were typical of how a canine and a human being act in an emergency, when the danger that threatens is heard, and not seen. In Robin's case it had impelled him to seek safety in silent and rapid retreat; whereas in my case it had the effect of glueing my feet to the ground and making retreat – rapid or otherwise – impossible.

When I had satisfied Robin that he was not to blame for our temporary separation, and his small body had stopped trembling, I put him down and together we walked up to where the leopard, who had put up such a game fight, and had so nearly won the last round, was lying dead.

I have told you the story, and while I have been telling it Robin – the biggest-hearted and the most faithful friend man ever had – has gone to the Happy Hunting Grounds, where I know I shall find him waiting for me.

THE CHOWGARH TIGERS

T he map of Eastern Kumaon that hangs on the wall before me is marked with a number of crosses, and below each cross is a date. These crosses indicate the locality, and the date, of the officially recorded human victims of the man-eating tiger of Chowgarh. There are sixty-four crosses on the map. I do not claim this as being a correct tally, for the map was posted up by me for two years, and during this period all kills were not reported to me; further, victims who were only mauled, and who died subsequently, have not been awarded a cross and a date.

The first cross is dated 15 December 1925, and the last, 21 March 1930. The distance between the extreme crosses, north to south, is fifty miles, and east to west, thirty miles, an area of 1,500 square miles of mountain and vale when the snow lies deep during winter and the valleys are scorching hot in summer. Over this area the Chowgarh tiger had established a reign of terror. Villages of varying size, some with a population of a hundred or more, and others with only a small family or two, are scattered throughout the area. Footpaths, beaten hard by bare feet, connect the villages. Some of these paths pass through thick forests, and when a man-eater renders their passage dangerous, inter-village communication is carried on by shouting. Standing on a commanding point, maybe a big rock or the roof of a house, a man cooees to attract the attention of the people in a neighbouring village, and when the cooee is answered the message is shouted across in a high-pitched voice. From village to village the message is tossed, and is broadcast throughout large areas in an incredibly short space of time.

It was at a District Conference in February 1929 that I found myself committed to have a try for this tiger. There were at that time three man-eaters in the Kumaon Division, and as the Chowgarh tiger had done most damage I promised to go in pursuit of it first.

The map with the crosses and dates, furnished to me by Government, showed that the man-eater was most active in the villages on the north and east face of the Kala Agar ridge. This ridge, some forty miles in length, rises to a height of 8,500 feet and is thickly wooded along the crest. A forest road runs along the north face of the ridge, in some places passing for miles through dense forests of oak and rhododendron, and in others forming a boundary between the forest and cultivated land. In one place the road forms a loop, and in this loop is situated the Kala Agar Forest Bungalow. This bungalow was my objective, and after a four days' march, culminating in a stiff climb of 4,000 feet, I arrived at it one evening in April 1929. The last human victim in this area was a young man of twenty-two, who had been killed while out grazing cattle, and while I was having breakfast, the morning after my arrival, the grandmother of the young man came to see me.

She informed me that the man-eater had, without any provocation, killed the only relative she had in the world. After giving me her grandson's history from the day he was born, and extolling his virtues, she pressed me to accept her three milch buffaloes to use as bait for the tiger, saying that if l killed the tiger with the help of her buffaloes she would have the satisfaction of feeling that she had assisted

HUMAN BEINGS KILLED BY THE CHOWGARH MAN-EATER

Village	Number
THALI	1
DEBOURA	1
BARHON	2
CHAMOLI	6
KAHOR	1
AM	2
DALKANIA	7
LOHAK	8
AHGAURA	2
PAHARPAN1	1
PADAMPURI	2
TANDA	1
NESORIYA	1
JHANGAON	1
KABRAGAON	1
KALA AGAR	8
RIKHAKOT	1
MATELA	3
KUNDAL	3
BABYAR	1
KHANSIUN	1
GARGARI	1
HAIRAKHAN	2
UKHALDHUNGA	1
PAKHARI	1
DUNGARI	2
GALNI	3
IOTAL	**64**

ANNUAL TOTALS

1926	15 KILLED
1927	9 KILLED
1928	14 KILLED
1929	17 KILLED
1930	9 KILLED
TOTAL	**64 KILLED**

in avenging her grandson. These full-grown animals were of no use to me, but knowing that refusal to accept them would give offence, I thanked the old lady and assured her I would draw on her for bait as soon as I had used up the four young male buffaloes I had brought with me from Naini Tai. The Headmen of nearby villages had now assembled, and from them I learned that the tiger had last been seen ten days previously in a village twenty miles away, on the eastern slope of the ridge, where it had killed and eaten a man and his wife.

A trail ten days old was not worth following up, and after a long discussion with the Headman I decided to make for Dalkania village on the eastern side of the ridge Dalkania is ten miles from Kala Agar, and about the same distance from the village where the man and his wife had been killed.

From the number of crosses Dalkania and the villages adjoining it had earned, it appeared that the tiger had its headquarters in the vicinity of these villages.

After breakfast next morning I left Kala Agar and followed the forest road, which I was informed would take me to the end of the ridge, where I should have to leave the road and take a path two miles downhill to Dalkania. This road, running right to the end of the ridge through dense forest, was very little used, and, examining it for tracks as I went along, I arrived at the point where the path took off at about 2 p.m. Here I met a number of men from Dalkania. They had heard – via the cooee method of communication – of my intention of camping at their village and had come up to the ridge to inform me that the tiger had that morning attacked a party of women, while they had been cutting their crops in a village ten miles to the north of Dalkania.

The men carrying my camp equipment had done eight

miles and were quite willing to carry on, but on learning from the villagers that the path to this village, ten miles away, was very rough and ran through dense forest, I decided to send my men with the villagers to Dalkania, and visit the scene of the tiger's attack alone. My servant immediately set about preparing a substantial meal for me, and at 3 p.m., having fortified myself, I set out on my ten-mile walk. Ten miles under favourable conditions is a comfortable two-and-a-half hours' walk, but here the conditions were anything but favourable. The track running along the east face of the hill wound in and out through deep ravines and was bordered alternately by rocks, dense undergrowth, and trees; and when every obstruction capable of concealing sudden death, in the form of a hungry maneater, had to be approached with caution, progress was of necessity slow. I was still several miles from my objective when the declining day warned me it was time to call a halt.

In any other area, sleeping under the stars on a bed of dry leaves would have ensured a restful night, but here, to sleep on the ground would have been to court death in a very unpleasant form. Long practice in selecting a suitable tree, and the ability to dispose myself comfortably in it have made sleeping up aloft a simple matter. On this occasion I selected an oak-tree, and, with the rifle tied securely to a branch, had been asleep for some hours when I was awakened by the rustling of several animals under the tree. The sound moved on, and presently I heard the scraping of claws on bark and realized that a family of bears were climbing some *karphal*[1] trees I had noticed growing a little

---

1 *Karphal is found on our hills at an elevation of 6,000 feet. The tree grows to a height of about forty feet and produces a small red and very sweet berry, which is greatly fancied by both human beings and bears.*

way down the hill-side. Bears are very quarrelsome when feeding, and sleep was impossible until they had eaten their fill and moved on.

The sun had been up a couple of hours when I arrived at the village, which consisted of two huts and a cattle-shed in a clearing of five acres surrounded by forest. The small community were in a state of terror and were overjoyed to see me. The wheatfield, a few yards from the huts, where the tiger, belly to ground, had been detected only just in time, stalking the three women cutting the crop, was eagerly pointed out to me. The man who had seen the tiger, and given the alarm, told me the tiger had retreated into the jungle, where it had been joined by a second tiger, and that the two animals had gone down the hill-side into the valley below. The occupants of the two huts had had no sleep, for the tigers, balked of their prey, had called at short intervals throughout the night, and had only ceased calling a little before my arrival. This statement, that there were two tigers, confirmed the reports I had already received that the man-eater was accompanied by a full-grown cub.

Our hill folk are very hospitable, and when the villagers learned that I had spent the night in the jungle, and that my camp was at Dalkania, they offered to prepare a meal for me. This I knew would strain the resources of the small community, so I asked for a dish of tea, but as there was no tea in the village I was given a drink of fresh milk sweetened to excess with jaggery, a very satisfying and not unpleasant drink – when one gets used to it. At the request of my hosts I mounted guard while the remaining portion of the wheat crop was cut; and at midday, taking the good wishes of the people with me, I went down into the valley in the direction in which the tigers had been heard calling.

The valley, starting from the watershed of the three rivers Ladhya, Nandhour, and Eastern Goula, runs south-west for twenty miles and is densely wooded. Tracking was impossible, and my only hope of seeing the tigers was to attract them to myself, or helped by the jungle folk to stalk them.

To those of you who may be inclined to indulge in the sport of man-eater hunting on foot, it will be of interest to know that the birds and animals of the jungle, and the four winds of heaven, play a very important part in this form of sport. This is not the place to give the names of the jungle folk on whose alarm-calls the sportsman depends, to a great extent, for his safety and knowledge of his quarry's movements; for in a country in which a walk up or down hill of three or four miles might mean a difference in altitude of as many thousand feet, the variation in fauna, in a well-stocked area, is considerable. The wind, however, at all altitudes, remains a constant factor, and a few words relevant to its importance in connexion with man-eater hunting on foot will not be out of place.

Tigers do not know that human beings have no sense of smell, and when a tiger becomes a man-eater it treats human beings exactly as it treats wild animals, that is, it approaches its intended victims up-wind, or lies up in wait for them down-wind.

The significance of this will be apparent when it is realized that, while the sportsman is trying to get a sight of the tiger, the tiger in all probability is trying to stalk the sportsman, or is lying up in wait for him. The contest, owing to the tiger's height, colouring, and ability to move without making a sound, would be very unequal were it not for the wind-factor operating in favour of the sportsman.

In all cases where killing is done by stalking or stealth, the victim is approached from behind. This being so, it would be suicidal for the sportsman to enter dense jungle, in which he had every reason to believe a man-eater was lurking, unless he was capable of making full use of the currents of air. For example, assuming that the sportsman has to proceed, owing to the nature of the ground, in the direction from which the wind is blowing, the danger would lie behind him, where he would be least able to deal with it, but by frequently tacking across the wind he could keep the danger alternately to right and left of him. In print this scheme may not appear very attractive, but in practice it works, and, short of walking backwards, I do not know of a better or safer method of going up-wind through dense cover in which a hungry man-eater is lurking.

By evening I had reached the upper end of the valley, without having seen the tigers and without having received any indication from birds or animal of their presence in the jungle. The only habitation then in sight was a cattle-shed, high up on the north side of the valley.

I was careful in the selection of a tree on this second night, and was rewarded by an undisturbed night's rest. Not long after dark the tigers called, and a few minutes later two shots from a muzzle-loader came echoing down the valley, followed by a lot of shouting from the graziers at the cattle-station. Thereafter the night was silent.

By the afternoon of the following day I had explored every bit of the valley, and I was making my way up a grassy slope intent on rejoining my men at Dalkania when I heard a long-drawn-out cooee from the direction of the cattle-shed. The cooee was repeated once and again, and on my sending back an answering call I saw a man climb on a projecting rock, and from this vantage point he shouted across the valley to ask if I was the sahib who had come from Naini Tal to shoot the man-eater. On my telling him I was that sahib, he informed me that his cattle had stampeded out of a ravine on my side of the valley at about midday, and that when he counted them on arrival at the cattle-station he found that one – a white cow – was missing.

He suspected that the cow had been killed by the tigers he had heard calling the previous night, half a mile to the west of where I was standing. Thanking him for his information, I set off to investigate the ravine. I had gone but a short distance along the edge of the ravine when I came on the tracks of the stampeding cattle, and following these tracks back I had no difficulty in finding the spot where the cow had been killed. After killing the cow the tigers had taken it down the steep hill-side into the ravine. An approach along the drag was not advisable, so going down into the valley I made a wide detour, and approached the spot where I expected the kill to be from the other side of the ravine. This side of the ravine was less steep than the side down which the kill had been taken, and was deep in young bracken – ideal ground for stalking over. Step by step, and as silently as a shadow, I made my way through the bracken, which reached above my waist, and when I was some thirty yards from the bed of the ravine a movement in front of me caught my eye. A white leg was suddenly thrust up into the air and violently agitated, and next moment there was a deep – throated growl – the tigers were on the kill and were having a difference of opinion over some toothful morsel.

For several minutes I stood perfectly still; the leg continued to be agitated, but the growl was not repeated. A nearer approach was not advisable, for even if I succeeded in covering the thirty yards without being seen, and managed to kill one of the tigers, the other, as likely as not, would blunder into me, and the ground I was on would give me no chance of defending myself. Twenty yards to my left front, and about the same distance from the tigers, there was an outcrop of rock, some ten to fifteen feet high. If I could reach this rock without being seen, I should in all probability get an easy shot at the tigers. Dropping on hands and knees, and pushing the rifle before me, I crawled through the bracken to the shelter of the rock, paused a minute to regain my breath and make quite sure the rifle was loaded, and then climbed the rock. When my eyes were level with the top, I looked over, and saw the two tigers.

One was eating at the hind quarters of the cow, while the other was lying near by licking its paws. Both tigers appeared to be about the same size, but the one that was licking its paws was several shades lighter than the other; and concluding that her light colouring was due to age and that she was the old man-eater, I aligned the sights very carefully on her, and fired. At my shot she reared up and fell backwards, while the other bounded down the ravine and was out of sight before I could press the second trigger. The tiger I had shot did not move again, and after pelting it with stones to make sure it was dead, I approached and met with a great disappointment; for a glance at close quarters showed me I had made a mistake and shot the cub – a mistake that during the ensuing twelve months cost the district fifteen lives and incidentally nearly cost me my own life.

Disappointment was to a certain extent mitigated by the thought that this young tigress, even if she had not actually killed any human beings herself, had probably assisted her old mother to kill (this assumption I later found to be correct), and in any case, having been nurtured on human flesh, she could – to salve my feelings – be classed as a potential man-eater.

Skinning a tiger with assistance on open ground and with the requisite appliances is an easy job, but here the job was anything but easy, for I was alone, surrounded by thick cover, and my only appliance was a penknife; and though there was no actual danger to be apprehended from the man-eater, for tigers never kill in excess of their requirements, there was the uneasy feeling in the back of my mind that the tigress had returned and was watching my every movement.

The sun was near setting before the arduous task was completed, and as I should have to spend yet another night in the jungle I decided to remain where I was. The tigress was a very old animal, as I could see from her pug-marks, and having lived all her life in a district in which there are nearly as many fire-arms as men to use them, had nothing to learn about men and their ways. Even so, there was just a chance that she might return to the kill some time during the night, and remain in the vicinity until light came in the morning.

My selection of a tree was of necessity limited, and the one I spent that night in proved, by morning, to be the most uncomfortable tree I have ever spent twelve hours in. The tigress called at intervals throughout the night, and as morning drew near the calling became fainter and fainter, and eventually died away on the ridge above me.

Cramped, and stiff, and hungry – I had been without food for sixty-four hours – and with my clothes clinging to me – it had rained for an hour during the night – I descended from the tree when objects were clearly visible, and, after tying the tiger's skin up in my coat, set off for Dalkania.

I have never weighed a tiger's skin when green, and if the skin, plus the head and paws, which I carried for fifteen miles that day weighed forty pounds at the start, I would have taken my oath it weighed two hundred pounds before I reached my destination.

In a courtyard flagged with great slabs of blue slate and common to a dozen houses, I found my men in conference with a hundred or more villagers. My approach, along a yard-wide lane between two houses, had not been observed, and the welcome I received when, bedraggled and covered with blood, I staggered into the circle of squatting men will live in my memory as long as memory lasts.

My forty-pound tent had been pitched in a field of stubble a hundred yards from the village, and I had hardly reached it before tea was laid out for me on a table improvised out of a couple of suit-cases and planks borrowed from the village. I was told later by the villagers that my men, who had been with me for years and had accompanied me on several similar expeditions, refusing to believe that the man-eater had claimed me as a victim, had kept a kettle on the boil night and day in anticipation of my return, and, further, had stoutly opposed the Headmen of Dalkania and the adjoining villages sending a report to Almora and Naini Tal that I was missing.

A hot bath, taken of necessity in the open and in full view of the village – I was too dirty and too tired to care who saw me – was followed by an ample dinner, and I was thinking of turning in for the night when a flash of lightning succeeded by a loud peal of thunder heralded the approach of a storm. Tent-pegs are of little use in a field, so long stakes were hurriedly procured and securely driven into the ground, and to these stakes the tent-ropes were tied. For further safety all the available ropes in camp were criss-crossed over the tent and lashed to the stakes. The storm of wind and rain lasted an hour and was one of the worst the little tent had ever weathered. Several of the guy-ropes were torn from the canvas, but the stakes and criss-cross ropes held. Most of my things were soaked through, and a little stream several inches deep was running from end to end of the tent; my bed, however, was comparatively dry, and by ten o'clock my men were safely lodged behind locked doors in the house the villagers had placed at their disposal, while I, with a loaded rifle for company, settled down to a sleep which lasted for twelve hours.

The following day was occupied in drying my kit and in cleaning and pegging out the tiger's skin. While these operations were in progress the villagers, who had taken a holiday from their field work, crowded round to hear my experiences and to tell me theirs. Every man present had lost one or more relatives, and several bore teeth and claw marks, inflicted by the man-eater, which they will carry to their graves. My regret at having lost an opportunity of killing the man-eater was not endorsed by the assembled men. True, there had originally been only one man-eater; but, of recent months, rescue parties who had gone out to recover the remains of human victims had found two tigers on the kills, and only a fortnight previously a man and his wife had been killed simultaneously, which was proof sufficient for them that both tigers were established man-eaters.

My tent was on a spur of the hill and commanded an extensive view. Immediately below me was the valley of the Nandhour River, with a hill, devoid of any cultivation, rising to a height of 9,000 feet on the far side. As I sat on the edge of the terraced fields that evening with a pair of good binoculars in my hand and the Government map spread out beside me, the villagers pointed out the exact positions where twenty human beings had been killed during the past three years. These kills were more or less evenly distributed over an area of forty square miles.

The forests in this area were open to grazing, and on the cattle-paths leading to them I decided to tie up my four young buffaloes.

During the following ten days no news was received of the tigress, and I spent the time in visiting the buffaloes in the morning, searching the forests in the day, and tying out the buffaloes in the evening. On the eleventh day my hopes were raised by the report that a cow had been killed in a ravine on the hill above my tent. A visit to the kill, however, satisfied me the cow had been killed by an old leopard, whose pug-marks I had repeatedly seen. The villagers complained that the leopard had for several years been taking heavy toll of their cattle and goats, so I decided to sit up for him. A shallow cave close to the dead cow gave me the cover I needed. I had not been Jong in the cave when I caught sight of the leopard coming down the opposite side of the ravine, and I was raising my rifle for a shot when I heard a very agitated voice from the direction of the village calling to me.

There could be but one reason for this urgent call, and grabbing up my hat I dashed out of the cave, much to the consternation of the leopard, who first flattened himself out on the ground, and then with an angry woof went bounding back the way he had come, while I scrambled up my side of the ravine; and, arriving at the top, shouted to the man that I was coming, and set off at top speed to join him.

The man had run all the way uphill from the village, and when he regained his breath he informed me that a woman had just been killed by the man-eater, about half a mile on the far side of the village. As we ran down the hill-side I saw a crowd of people collected in the courtyard already alluded to. Once again my approach through the narrow lane was not observed, and looking over the heads of the assembled men, I saw a girl sitting on the ground.

The upper part of her clothing had been torn off her young body, and with head thrown back and hands resting on the ground behind to support her, she sat without sound or movement, other than the heaving up and down of her breast, in the hollow of which the blood that was flowing down her face and neck was collecting in a sticky congealed mass.

My presence was soon detected and a way made for me to approach the girl. While I was examining her wounds, a score of people, all talking at the same time, informed me that the attack on the girl had been made on comparatively open ground in full view of a number of people, including the girl's husband; that alarmed at their combined shouts the tiger had left the girl and gone off in the direction of the forest; that leaving the girl for dead where she had fallen her companions had run back to the village to inform me; that subsequently the girl had regained consciousness and returned to the village; that she would without doubt die of her injuries in a few minutes; and that they would then carry her back to the scene of the attack, and I could sit up over her corpse and shoot the tiger.

While this information was being imparted to me

the girl's eyes never left my face and followed my every movement with the liquid pleading gaze of a wounded and frightened animal. Room to move unhampered, quiet to collect my wits, and clean air for the girl to breathe were necessary, and I am afraid the methods I employed to gain them were not as gentle as they might have been. When the last of the men had left in a hurry, I set the women, who up to now had remained in the background, to warming water and to tearing my shirt, which was comparatively clean and dry, into bandages, while one girl, who appeared to be on the point of getting hysterics, was bundled off to scour the village for a pair of scissors. The water and bandages were ready before the girl I had sent for the scissors returned with the only pair, she said, the village could produce. They had been found in the house of a tailor, long since dead, and had been used by the widow for digging up potatoes. The rusty blades, some eight inches long, could not be made to meet at any point, and after a vain attempt I decided to leave the thick coils of blood-caked hair alone.

The major wounds consisted of two claw cuts, one starting between the eyes and extending right over the head and down to the nape of the neck, leaving the scalp hanging in two halves, and the other, starting near the first, running across the forehead up to the right ear. In addition to these ugly gaping wounds there were a number of deep scratches on the right breast, right shoulder and neck, and one deep cut on the back of the right hand, evidently inflicted when the girl had put up her hand in a vain attempt to shield her head.

A doctor friend whom I had once taken out tiger-shooting on foot had, on our return after an exciting morning, presented me with a two-ounce bottle of yellow fluid which he advised me to carry whenever I went out shooting. I had carried the bottle in the inner pocket of my shooting-jacket for over a year and a portion of the fluid had evaporated; but the bottle was still three-part full, and after I had washed the girl's head and body I knocked the neck off the bottle and poured the contents, to the last drop, into the wounds. This done I bandaged the head, to try to keep the scalp in position, and then picked up the girl and carried her to her home – a single room combining living-quarters, kitchen, and nursery – with the women following behind.

Dependent from a rafter near the door was an open basket, the occupant of which was now clamouring to be fed. This was a complication with which I could not deal, so I left the solution of it to the assembled women. Ten days later, when on the eve of my departure I visited the girl for the last time, I found her sitting on the doorstep of her home with the baby asleep in her lap.

Her wounds, except for a sore at the nape of her neck where the tiger's claws had sunk deepest into the flesh, were all healed, and when parting her great wealth of raven-black hair to show me where the scalp had made a perfect join, she said, with a smile, that she was very glad her young sister had – quite by mistake – borrowed the wrong pair of scissors from the tailor's widow (for a shorn head here is the sign of widowhood). If these lines should ever be read by my friend the doctor I should like him to know that the little bottle of yellow fluid he so thoughtfully provided for me saved the life of a very brave young mother.

While I had been attending to the girl my men had procured a goat. Following back the blood trail made by the girl I found the spot where the attack had taken place, and tying the goat to a bush I climbed into a stunted oak, the only tree in the vicinity, and prepared for an all-night vigil. Sleep, even in snatches, was not possible, for my seat was only a few feet from the ground, and the tigress was still without her dinner. However, I neither saw nor heard anything throughout the night.

On examining the ground in the morning – I had not had time to do this the previous evening – I found that the tigress, after attacking the girl, had gone up the valley for half a mile to where a cattle-track crossed the Nandhour River. This track it had followed for two miles, to its junction with the forest road on the ridge above Dalkania. Here on the hard ground I lost the tracks.

For two days the people in all the surrounding villages kept as close to their habitations as the want of sanitary conveniences permitted, and then on the third day news was brought to me by four runners that the man-eater had claimed a victim at Lohali, a village five miles to the south of Dalkania. The runners stated that the distance by the forest road was ten miles, but only five by a short cut by which they proposed taking me back. My preparations were soon made, and a little after midday I set off with my four guides.

A very stiff climb of two miles brought us to the crest of the long ridge south of Dalkania and in view of the valley three miles below, where the 'kill' was reported to have taken place. My guides could give me no particulars. They lived in a small village a mile on the near side of Lohali, and at 10 a.m. a message had come to them – in the manner already described – that a woman of Lohali had been killed by the man-eater, and they were instructed to convey this information to me at Dalkania.

The top of the hill on which we were standing was bare of trees, and, while I regained my breath and had a smoke, my companions pointed out the landmarks. Close to where we were resting, and under the shelter of a great rock, there was a small ruined hut, with a circular thorn enclosure near by. Questioned about this hut, the men told me the following story. Four years previously a Bhutia (a man from across the border), who had all the winter been sending packages of *gur*, salt, and other commodities from the bazaars at the foot-hills into the interior of the district, had built the hut with the object of resting and fattening his flock of goats through the summer and rains, and getting them fit for the next winter's work. After a few weeks the goats wandered down the hill and damaged my informants' crops, and when they came up to lodge a protest, they found the hut empty, and the fierce sheep-dog these men invariably keep with them, to guard their camps at night, chained to an iron stake and dead. Foul play was suspected, and next day men were collected from adjoining villages and a search organized. Pointing to an oak-tree scored by lightning and distant some four hundred yards, my informants said that under it the remains of the man – his skull and a few splinters of bone – and his clothes had been found. This was the Chowgarh man-eater's first human victim.

There was no way of descending the precipitous hill from where we were sitting, and the men informed me we should have to proceed half a mile along the ridge to where we should find a very steep and rough track which would take us straight down, past their village, to Lohali, which we could see in the valley below. We had covered about half the distance we had to go along the ridge, when all at once, and without being able to ascribe any reason for it, I felt we were being followed. Arguing with myself against this feeling was of no avail; there was only one man-eater in all this area and she had procured a kill three miles away which she was not likely to leave. However, the uneasy feeling persisted, and as we were now at the widest part of the grassy ridge, I made the men sit down, instructing them not to move until I returned, and myself set out on a tour of investigation. Retracing my steps to where we had first come out on the ridge, I entered the jungle, and carefully worked round the open ground and back to where the men were sitting. No alarm-call of animal or bird indicated that a tiger was anywhere in the vicinity, but from there on I made the four men walk in front of me, while I brought up the rear, with thumb on safety-catch and a constant look-out behind.

When we arrived at the little village my companions had started from, they asked for permission to leave me. I was very glad of this request, for I had a mile of dense scrub jungle to go through, and though the feeling that I was being followed had long since left me, I felt safer and more comfortable with only my own life to guard. A little below the outlying terraced fields, and where the dense scrub started, there was a crystal-clear spring of water, from which the village drew its water-supply. Here in the soft wet ground I found the fresh pug-marks of the man-eater.

These pug-marks, coming from the direction of the village I was making for, coupled with the uneasy feeling I had experienced on the ridge above, convinced me that something had gone wrong with the 'kill' and that my quest would be fruitless. As I emerged from the scrub jungle I came in view of Lohali, which consisted of five or six small houses. Near the door of one of these houses a group of people were collected.

My approach over the steep open ground and narrow terraced fields was observed, and a few men detached themselves from the group near the door and advanced to meet me. One of the number, an old i:p.an, bent down to touch my feet, and with tears streaming down his cheeks implored me to save the life of his daughter. His story was as short as it was tragic. His daughter, who was a widow and the only relative he had in the world, had gone out at about ten o'clock to collect dry sticks with which to cook their midday meal. A small stream flows through the valley, and on the far side of the stream from the village the hill goes steeply up. On the lower slope of this hill there are a few terraced fields. At the edge of the lowest field, and distant about a hundred and fifty yards from the home, the woman had started to collect sticks. A little later, some women who were washing their clothes in the stream heard a scream, and on looking up saw the woman and a tiger disappearing together into the dense thorn bushes, which extended from the edge of the field right down to the stream. Dashing back to the village, the women raised an alarm. The frightened villagers made no attempt at a rescue, and a message for help was shouted to a village higher up the valley, from where it was tossed back to the village from which the four men had set out to find me. Half an hour after the message had been sent, the wounded woman crawled home. Her story was that she had seen the tiger just as it was about to spring on her, and as there was no time to run, she had jumped down the almost perpendicular hill-side and while she was in the air the tiger had caught her and they had gone down the hill together. She remembered nothing further until she regained consciousness and found herself near the stream; and being unable to call for help, she had crawled back to the village on her hands and knees.

We had reached the door of the house while this tale was being told. Making the people stand back from the door – the only opening in the four walls of the room – I drew the blood-stained sheet off the woman, whose pitiful condition I am not going to attempt to describe. Had I been a qualified doctor, armed with modern appliances, instead of just a mere man with a little permanganate of potash in his pocket, I do not think it would have been possible to have saved the woman's life; for the deep tooth and claw wounds in her face, neck, and other parts of her body had, in that hot, unventilated room, already turned septic. Mercifully &he was only semi-conscious. The old father had followed me into the room, and, more for his satisfaction than for any good I thought it would do, I washed the caked blood from the woman's head and body, and cleaned out the wounds as best I could with my handkerchief and a strong solution of permanganate.

It was now too late to think of returning to my camp, and a place would have to be found in which to pass the night. A little way up the stream, and not far from where the women had been washing their clothes, there was a giant pipal-tree, with a foot-high masonry platform round it used by the villagers for religious ceremonies.

I undressed on the platform and bathed in the stream; and when the wind had carried out the functions of a towel, dressed again, put my back to the tree and, laying the loaded rifle by my side, prepared to see the night out. Admittedly it was an unsuitable place in which to spend the night, but any place was preferable to the village and that dark room, with its hot fetid atmosphere and swarm of buzzing flies, where a woman in torment fought desperately for breath.

During the night the wailing of women announced that the sufferer's troubles were over, and when I passed through the village at daybreak preparations for the funeral were well advanced.

From the experience of this unfortunate woman, and that of the girl at Dalkania, it was now evident that the old tigress had depended, to a very great extent, on her cub to kill the human beings she attacked. Usually only one out of every hundred people attacked by man-eating tigers escapes, but in the case of this man-eater it was apparent that more people would be mauled than killed outright, and as the nearest hospital was fifty miles away, when I returned to Naini Tal I appealed to Government to send a supply of disinfectants and dressings to all the Headmen of villages in the area in which the man-eater was operating. On my subsequent visit I was glad to learn that the request had been complied with, and that the disinfectants had saved the lives of a number of people.

I stayed at Dalkania for another week and announced on a Saturday that I would leave for home the following Monday. I had now been in the man-eater's domain for close on a month, and the constant strain of sleeping in an open tent, and of walking endless miles during the day with the prospect of every step being the last, was beginning to tell on my nerves. The villagers received my announcement with consternation, and only desisted from trying to make me change my decision when I promised them I would return at the first opportunity.

After breakfast on Sunday morning the Headman of Dalkania paid me a visit and requested me to shoot them some game before I left. The request was gladly acceded to, and half an hour later, accompanied by four villagers and one of my own men, and armed with a .275 rifle and a clip of cartridges, I set off for the hill on the far side of the Nandhour River, on the upper slopes of which I had, from my camp, frequently seen ghooral feeding.

One of the villagers accompanying me was a tall gaunt man with a terribly disfigured face. He had been a constant visitor to my camp, and finding in me a good listener had told and re-told his encounter with the man-eater so often that I could, without effort, repeat the whole story in my sleep. The encounter had taken place four years previously, and is best told in his own words.

'Do you see that pine-tree, sahib, at the bottom of the grassy slope on the shoulder of the hill? Yes, the pine-tree with a big white rock to the east of it. Well, it was at the upper edge of the grassy slope that the man-eater attacked me. The grassy slope is as perpendicular as the wall of a house, and none but a hillman could find foot-hold on it. My son, who was eight years of age at the time, and I had cut grass on that slope on the day of my misfortune, carrying the grass up in armfuls to the belt of trees where the ground is level.

'I was stooping down at the very edge of the slope, tying the grass into a big bundle, when the tiger sprang at me and buried its teeth, one under my right eye, one in my chin, and the other two here at the back of my neck. The tiger's mouth struck me with a great blow and I fell over on my back, while the tiger lay on top of me chest to chest, with its stomach between my legs. When falling backwards I had flung out my arms and my right hand had come in contact with an oak-sapling. As my fingers grasped the sapling, an idea came to me. My legs were free, and if I could draw them up and insert my feet under and against the tiger's belly, I might be able to push the tiger off: and run away. The pain, as the tiger crushed all the bones on the right side of my face, was terrible; but I did not lose consciousness, but you see, sahib, at that time I was a young man, and in all the hills there was no one to compare with me in strength. Very slowly, so as not to anger the tiger, I drew my legs up on either side of it, and gently, very gently, inserted my bare feet against its belly. Then placing my left hand against its chest and pushing and kicking upwards with all my might, I lifted the tiger right off the ground and, we being on the very edge of the perpendicular hill-side, the tiger went crashing down and belike would have taken me with him, had my hold on the sapling not been a good one.

'My son had been too frightened to run away, and when the tiger had gone, I took his loincloth from him and wrapped it round my head, and holding his hand I walked back to the village. Arrived at my home I told my wife to call all my friends together, for I wished to see their faces before I died. When my friends were assembled and saw my condition, they wanted to put me on a charpoy and carry me fifty miles to the Almora hospital, but this I would not consent to; for my suffering was great, and being assured that my time had come, I wanted to die where I had been born, and where I had lived all my life. Water was brought, for I was thirsty and my head was on fire, but when it was poured into my mouth, it all flowed out through the holes in my neck. Thereafter, for a period beyond measure, there was great confusion in my mind, and much pain in my head and in my neck, and while I waited and longed for death to end my sufferings my wounds healed of themselves, and I became well.

'And now, sahib, I am as you see me, old and thin, and with white hair, and a face that no man can look on without repulsion. My enemy lives and continues to claim victims; but do not be deceived into thinking it is a tiger, for it is no tiger but an evil spirit, who, when it craves for human flesh and blood, takes on for a little while the semblance of a tiger. But they say you are a sadhu, sahib, and the spirits that guard sadhus are more powerful than this evil spirit, as is proved by the fact that you spent three days and three nights alone in the jungle, and came out – as your men said you would – alive and unhurt.'

Looking at the great frame of the man, it was easy to picture him as having been a veritable giant. And a giant in strength he must have been, for no man, unless he had been endowed with strength far above the average, could have lifted the tigress into the air, torn its hold from the side of his head, carrying away, as it did, half his face with it, and hurled it down the precipitous hill.

My gaunt friend constituted himself our guide, and with a beautifully polished axe, with long tapering handle, over his shoulder, led us by devious steep paths to the valley below. Fording the Nandhour River, we crossed several wide terraced fields, now gone out of cultivation for fear of the man-eater, and on reaching the foot of the hill started what proved to be a very stiff climb, through forest, to the grass slopes above. Gaunt my friend may have been, but he lacked nothing in wind, and tough as I was, it was only by calling frequent halts – to admire the view – that I was able to keep up with him.

Emerging from the tree forest, we went diagonally across the grassy slope, in the direction of a rock cliff that extended upwards for a thousand feet or more. It was on this cliff, sprinkled over with tufts of short grass, that I had seen ghooral feeding from my tent. We had covered a few hundred yards when one of these small mountain-goats started up out of a ravine, and at my shot crumpled up and slipped back out of sight. Alarmed by the report of the rifle, another ghooral, that had evidently been lying asleep at the foot of the cliff, sprang to his feet and went up the rock face, as only he or his big brother the tahr could have done. As he climbed upwards, I lay down and, putting the sight to two hundred yards, waited for him to stop. This he presently did, coming out on a projecting rock to look down on us. At my shot he staggered, regained his footing, and very slowly continued his climb. At the second shot he fell, hung for a second or two on a narrow ledge, and then fell through space to the grassy slope whence he had started. Striking the ground he rolled over and over, passing within a hundred yards of us, and eventually came to rest on a cattle-track a hundred and fifty yards below.

I have only once, in all the years I have been shooting, witnessed a similar sight to the one we saw during the next few minutes, and on that occasion the marauder was a leopard.

The ghooral had hardly come to rest when a big Himalayan bear came lumbering out of a ravine on the far side of the grassy slope and, with never a pause or backward look, came at a fast trot along the cattle-track. On reaching the dead goat he sat down and took it into his lap, and as he started nosing the goat, I fired. Maybe I hurried over my shot, or allowed too much for refraction; anyway the bullet went low and struck the bear in the stomach instead of in the chest. To the six of us who were intently watching, it appeared that the bear took the smack of the bullet as an assault from the ghooral, for, rearing up, he flung the animal from him and came galloping along the track, emitting angry grunts. As he passed a hundred yards below us I fired my fifth and last cartridge, the bullet, as I found later, going through the fleshy part of his hind quarters.

While the men retrieved the two ghooral, I descended to examine the blood trail. The blood on the track showed the bear to be hard hit, but even so there was danger in following it up with an empty rifle, for bears are bad-tempered at the best of times, and are very ugly customers to deal with when wounded.

When the men rejoined me a short council of war was held. Camp was three and a half miles away, and as it was now 2 p.m. it would not be possible to fetch more ammunition, track down and kill the bear, and get back home by dark; so it was unanimously decided that we should follow up the wounded animal and try to finish it off with stones and the axe.

The hill was steep and fairly free of undergrowth, and by keeping above the bear there was a sporting chance of our being able to accomplish our task without serious mishap. We accordingly set off, I leading the way, followed by three men, the rear being brought up by two men each with a ghooral strapped to his back. Arrived at the spot where I had fired my last shot, additional blood on the track greatly encouraged us. Two hundred yards farther on, the blood trail led down into a deep ravine. Here we divided up our force, two men crossing to the far side, the owner of the axe and I remaining on the near side, with the men carrying the ghooral following in our rear. On the word being given we started to advance down the hill. In the bed of the ravine, and fifty feet below us, was a dense patch of stunted bamboo, and when a stone was thrown into this thicket, the bear got up with a scream of rage; and six men, putting their best foot foremost, went straight up the hill. I was not trained to this form of exercise, and on looking back to see if the bear was gaining on us, I saw, much to my relief, that he was going as hard downhill as we were going uphill. A shout to my companions, a rapid change of direction, and we were off in full cry and rapidly gaining on our quarry. A few well-aimed shots had been registered, followed by delighted shouts from the marksmen and angry grunts from the bear, when at a sharp bend in the ravine, which necessitated a cautious advance, we lost touch with the bear. To have followed the blood trail would have been easy, but here the ravine was full of big rocks, behind any of which the bear might have been lurking, so while the encumbered men sat down for a rest, a cast was made on either side of the ravine. While my companion went forward to look down into the ravine, I went to the right to prospect a rocky cliff that went sheer down for some two hundred feet. Holding to a tree for support, I leaned over and saw the bear lying on a narrow ledge forty feet immediately below me. I picked up a stone, about thirty pounds in weight, and, again advancing to the edge and in imminent danger of going over myself, I raised the stone above my head with both hands and hurled it.

The stone struck the ledge a few inches from the bear's head, and scrambling to his feet he disappeared from sight, to reappear a minute later on the side of the hill. Once again the hunt was on. The ground was here more open and less encumbered with rocks, and the four of us who were running light had no difficulty in keeping up with him. For a mile or more we ran him at top speed, until we eventually cleared the forest and emerged on to the terraced fields. Rain-water had cut several deep and narrow channels across the fields, and in one of these channels the bear took cover.

The man with the distorted face was the only armed member of the party and he was unanimously elected executioner. Nothing loath, he cautiously approached the bear and, swinging his beautifully polished axe aloft, brought the square head down on the bear's skull. The result was as alarming as it was unexpected. The axe-head rebounded off the bear's skull as though it had been struck on a block of rubber, and with a scream of rage the animal reared up on his hind legs. Fortunately he did not follow up his advantage, for we were bunched together, and in trying to run got in each other's way.

The bear did not appear to like this open ground, and after going a short way down the channel again took cover. It was now my turn for the axe. The bear, however, having once been struck, resented my approach, and it was only after a great deal of manoeuvring that I eventually got within striking distance. It had been my ambition when a boy to be a lumberman in Canada, and I had attained sufficient proficiency with an axe to split a matchstick. I had no fear, therefore, as the owner had, of the axe glancing off and getting damaged on the stones, and the moment I got within reach I buried the entire blade in the bear's skull.

Himalayan bearskins are very greatly prized by our hill folk, and the owner of the axe was a very proud and envied man when I told him he could have the skin in addition to a double share of the ghooral meat. Leaving the men, whose numbers were being rapidly augmented by new arrivals from the village, to skin and divide up the bag, I climbed up to the village and paid, as already related, a last visit to the injured girl. The day had been a strenuous one, and if the man-eater had paid me a visit that night she would have 'caught me napping'.

On the road I had taken when coming to Dalkania there were several long, stiff climbs up treeless hills, and when I mentioned the discomforts of this road to the villagers they had suggested that I should go back via Haira Khan. This route would necessitate only one climb to the ridge above the village, from where it was downhill all the way to Ranibagh, whence I could complete the journey to Naini Tal by car.

I had warned my men overnight to prepare for an early start, and a little before sunrise, leaving them to pack up and follow me, I said good-bye to my friends at Dalkania and started on the two-mile climb to the forest road on the ridge above. The footpath I took was not the one by which my men, and later I, had arrived at Dalkania, but was one the villagers used when going to, and returning from, the bazaars in the foot-hills.

The path wound in and out of deep ravines, through thick oak and pine forests and dense undergrowth. There had been no news of the tigress for a week. This absence of news made me all the more careful, and an hour after leaving camp I arrived without mishap at an open glade near the top of the hill, within a hundred yards of the forest road.

The glade was pear-shaped, roughly a hundred yards Jong and fifty yards wide, with a stagnant pool of rain-water in the centre of it. Sambur and other game used this pool as a drinking-place and wallow and, curious to see the tracks round it, I left the path, which skirted the left-hand side of the glade and passed close under a cliff of rock which extended up to the road. As I approached the pool I saw the pug-marks of the tigress in the soft earth at the edge of the water. She had approached the pool from the same direction as I had, and, evidently disturbed by me, had crossed the water and gone into the dense tree and scrub jungle on the right-hand side of the glade. A great chance lost, for had I kept as careful a look-out in front as I had behind I should have seen her before she saw me. However, though I had missed a chance, the advantages were now all on my side and distinctly in my favour.

The tigress had seen me, or she would not have crossed the pool and hurried for shelter, as her tracks showed she had done. Having seen me, she had also seen that I was alone, and watching me from cover as she undoubtedly was, she would assume I was going to the pool to drink as she had done. My movements up to this had been quite natural, and if l could continue to make her think I was unaware of her presence, she would possibly give me a second chance. Stooping down and keeping a very sharp look-out from under my hat, I coughed several times, splashed the water about, and then, moving very slowly and gathering dry sticks on the way, I went to the foot of the steep rock. Here I built a small fire, and putting my back to the rock lit a cigarette. By the time the cigarette had been smoked the fire had burnt out. I then lay down, and pillowing my head on my left arm placed the rifle on the ground with my finger on the trigger.

The rock above me was too steep for any animal to find foot-hold on. I had therefore only my front to guard, and as the heavy cover nowhere approached to within less than twenty yards of my position I was quite safe. I had all this time neither seen nor heard anything; nevertheless, I was convinced that the tigress was watching me. The rim of my hat, while effectually shading my eyes, did not obstruct my vision, and inch by inch I scanned every bit of the jungle within my range of view. There was not a breath of wind blowing, and not a leaf or blade of grass stirred. My men, whom I had instructed to keep close together and sing from the time they left camp until they joined me on the forest road, were not due for an hour and a half, and during this time it was more than likely that the tigress would break cover and try to stalk or rush me.

There are occasions when time drags, and others when it flies. My left arm, on which my head was pillowed, had long since ceased to prick and had gone dead, but even so the singing of the men in the valley below reached me all too soon. The voices grew louder, and presently I caught sight of the men as they rounded a sharp bend. It was possibly at this bend that the tigress had seen me as she turned round to re-trace her steps after having her drink. Another failure, and the last chance on this trip gone.

After my men had rested we climbed up to the road, and set off on what proved to be a very long twenty-mile march to the Forest Rest House at Haira Khan. After going a couple of hundred yards over open ground, the road entered very thick forest, and here I made the men walk in front while I brought up the rear. We had gone about two miles in this order, when on turning a corner I saw a man sitting on the road, herding buffaloes. It was now time to call a halt for breakfast, so I asked the man where we could get water. He pointed down the hill straight in front of him, and said there was a spring down there from which his village, which was just round the shoulder of the hill, drew its water-supply. There was, however, no necessity for us to go down the hill for water, for if we continued a little farther we should find a good spring on the road.

His village was at the upper end of the valley in which the woman of Lohali had been killed the previous week, and he told me that nothing had been heard of the man-eater since, and added that the animal was possibly now at the other end of the district. I disabused his mind on this point by telling him about the fresh pug-marks I had seen at the pool, and advised him very strongly to collect his buffaloes and return to the village. His buffaloes, some ten in number, were straggling up towards the road, and he said he would leave as soon as they had grazed up to where he was sitting. Handing him a cigarette, I left him with a final warning. What occurred after I left was related to me by the men of the village, when I paid the district a second visit some months later.

When the man eventually got home that day he told the assembled villagers of our meeting, and my warning, and said that after he had watched me go round a bend in the road a hundred yards away he started to light the cigarette I had given him. A wind was blowing, and to protect the flame of the match he bent forward, and while in this position he was seized from behind by the right shoulder and pulled backwards. His first thought was of the party who had just left him, but unfortunately his cry for help was not heard by them. Help, however, was near at hand, for as soon as the buffaloes heard his cry, mingled with the growl of the tigress, they charged on to the road and drove the tigress off. His shoulder and arm were broken, and with great difficulty he managed to climb on the back of one of his brave rescuers, and, followed by the rest of the herd, reached his home. The villagers tied up his wounds as best

they could and carried him thirty miles, non-stop, to the Haldwani hospital, where he died shortly after admission.

When Atropos, who snips the threads of life, misses one thread she cuts another, and we who do not know why one thread is missed and another cut call it Fate, Kismet, or what we will.

For a month I had lived in an open tent, a hundred yards from the nearest human being, and from dawn to dusk had wandered through the jungles, and on several occasions had disguised myself as a woman and cut grass in places where no local inhabitant dared to go. During this period the man-eater had, quite possibly, missed many opportunities of adding me to her bag and now, when making a final effort, she had quite by chance encountered this unfortunate man and claimed him as a victim.

II

The following February I returned to Dalkania. A number of human beings had been killed, and many more wounded, over a wide area since my departure from the district the previous summer, and as the whereabouts of the tigress was not known and the chances in one place were as good as in another, I decided to return and camp on the ground with which I was now familiar.

On my arrival at Dalkania I was told that a cow had been killed the previous evening, on the hill on which the bear hunt had taken place. The men who had been herding the cattle at the time were positive that the animal they had seen killing the cow was a tiger. The kill was lying near some bushes at the edge of a deserted field, and was clearly visible from the spot where my tent was being put up. Vultures were circling over the kill, and looking through my field-glasses I saw several of these birds perched on a tree, to the left of the kill. From the fact the kill was lying out in the open and the vultures had not descended on it, I concluded: (a) that the cow had been killed by a leopard, and (b) that the leopard was lying up close to the kill.

The ground below the field on which the cow was lying was very steep and overgrown with dense brushwood. The man-eater was still at large, and an approach over this ground was therefore inadvisable.

To the right was a grassy slope, but the ground here was too open to admit of my approaching the hill without being seen. A deep, heavily wooded ravine, starting from near the crest of the hill, ran right down to the Nandhour River, passing within a short distance of the kill. The tree on which the vultures were perched was growing on the edge of this ravine. I decided on this ravine as my line of approach. While I had been planning out the stalk with the assistance of the villagers, who knew every foot of the ground, my men had prepared tea for me. The day was now on the decline, but by going hard I should just have time to visit the kill and return to camp before nightfall.

Before setting off I instructed my men to be on the lookout. If, after hearing a shot, they saw me on the open ground near the kill, three or four of them were immediately to leave camp and, keeping to the open ground, to join me. On the other hand, if I did not fire, and failed to return by morning, a search party was to be organized.

The ravine was overgrown with raspberry bushes and strewn with great rocks, and as the wind was blowing down-hill, my progress was slow. After a stiff climb I eventually reached the tree on which the vultures were perched, only to find that the kill was not visible from this spot. The deserted field, which through my field-glasses had appeared to be quite straight, I found to be crescent-shaped, ten yards across at its widest part and tapering to a point at both ends. The outer edge was bordered with dense undergrowth, and the hill fell steeply away from the inner edge. Only two-thirds of the field was visible from where I was standing, and in order to see the remaining one-third, on which the kill was lying, it would be necessary either to make a wide detour and approach from the far side or climb the tree on which the vultures were perched.

I decided on the latter course. The cow, as far as I could judge, was about twenty yards from the tree, and it was quite possible that the animal that had killed her was even less than that distance from me. To climb the tree without disturbing the killer would have been an impossible feat, and would not have been attempted had it not been for the vultures. There were by now some twenty of these birds on the tree, and their number was being added to by new arrivals, and 'as the accommodation on the upper branches was limited there was much flapping of wings and quarrelling. The tree was leaning outwards away from the hill, and about ten feet from the ground a great limb projected out over the steep hill-side. Hampered with the rifle, I had great difficulty in reaching this limb. Waiting until a fresh quarrel had broken out among the vultures, I stepped out along the branch – a difficult balancing feat where a slip or false step would have resulted in a fall of a hundred or more feet on to the rocks below – reached a fork, and sat down.

The kill, from which only a few pounds of flesh had been eaten, was now in full view. I had been in position about ten minutes, and was finding my perch none too comfortable, when two vultures, who had been circling round and were uncertain of their reception on the tree, alighted on the field a short distance from the cow. They had hardly come to rest when they were on the wing again, and at the same moment the bushes on my side of the kill were gently agitated and out into the open stepped a fine male leopard.

Those who have never seen a leopard under favourable conditions in his natural surroundings can have no conception of the grace of movement, and beauty of colouring, of this the most graceful and the most beautiful of all animals in our Indian jungles. Nor are his attractions limited to outward appearances, for, pound for pound, his strength is second to none, and in courage he lacks nothing. To class such an animal as vermin, as is done in some parts of India, is a crime which only those could perpetrate whose knowledge of the leopard is limited to the miserable, underfed, and mangy specimens seen in captivity.

But beautiful as the specimen was that stood before me, his life was forfeit, for he had taken to cattle killing, and I had promised the people of Dalkania and other villages on my last visit that I would rid them of this their minor enemy, if opportunity offered. The opportunity had now come, and I do not think the leopard heard the shot that killed him.

Of the many incomprehensible things one meets with in life, the hardest to assign any reason for is the way in which misfortune dogs an individual, or a family. Take as an example the case of the owner of the cow over which I had shot the leopard. He was a boy, eight years of age, and an only child. Two years previously his mother, while out cutting grass for the cow, had been killed and eaten by the man-eater, and twelve months later his father had suffered a like fate. The few pots and pans the family possessed had been sold to pay off the small debt left by the father, and the son started life as the owner of one cow; and this particular cow the leopard had selected, out of a herd of two or three hundred head of village cattle, and killed. (I am afraid my attempt to repair a heart-break was not very successful in this case, for though the new cow, a red one, was an animal of parts, it did not make up to the boy for the loss of his lifelong white companion.)

My young buffaloes had been well cared for by the man in whose charge I had left them, and the day after my arrival I started tying them out, though I had little hope of the tigress's accepting them as bait.

Five miles down the Nandhour valley nestles a little village at the foot of a great cliff of rock, some thousand or more feet high. The man-eater had, during the past few months, killed four people on the outskirts of this village. Shortly after I shot the leopard, a deputation came from this village to request me to move my camp from Dalkania to a site that had been selected for me near their village. I was told that the tiger had frequently been seen on the cliff above the village and that it appeared to have its home in one of the many caves in the cliff face. That very morning, I was informed, some women out cutting grass had seen the tiger, and the villagers were now in a state of terror, and too frightened to leave their homes. Promising the deputation I would do all I could to help them, I made a very early start next morning, climbed the hill opposite the village, and scanned the cliff for an hour or more through my field-glasses. I then crossed the valley, and by way of a very deep ravine climbed the cliff above the village. Here the going was very difficult and not at all to my liking, for added to the danger of a fall, which would have resulted in a broken neck, was the danger of an attack on ground on which it would be impossible to defend oneself.

By 2 p.m. I had seen as much of the rock cliff as I shall ever want to see again, and was making my way up the valley towards my camp and breakfast, when on looking back before starting the stiff climb to Dalkania I saw two men running towards me from the direction in which I had just come. On joining me the men informed me that a tiger had just killed a bullock in the deep ravine up which I had gone earlier in the day. Telling one of the men to go on up to my camp and instruct my servant to send tea and some food, I turned round and, accompanied by the other man, re-traced my steps down the valley.

The ravine where the bullock had been killed was about two hundred feet deep and one hundred feet wide. As we approached it I saw a number of vultures rising, and when we arrived at the kill I found the vultures had cleaned it out, leaving only the skin and bones. The spot where the remains of the bullock were lying was only a hundred yards from the village, but there was no way up the steep bank, so my guide took me a quarter of a mile down the ravine, to where a cattle-track crossed it. This track, after gaining the high ground, wound in and out through dense scrub jungle before it finally fetched up at the village. On arrival at the village I told the Headman that the vultures had ruined the kill, and asked him to provide me with a young buffalo and a short length of stout rope; while these were being procured, two of my men arrived from Dalkania with the food I had sent for.

The sun was near setting when I re-entered the ravine, followed by several men leading a vigorous young male buffalo which the Headman had purchased for me from an adjoining village. Fifty yards from where the bullock had been killed, one end of a pine-tree washed down from the hill above had been buried deep in the bed of the ravine. After tying the buffalo very securely to the exposed end of the pine, the men returned to the village. There were no trees in the vicinity, and the only possible place for a sit-up was a narrow ledge on the village side of the ravine. With great difficulty I climbed to this ledge, which was about two feet wide by five feet long, and twenty feet above the bed of the ravine. From a little below the ledge, the rock shelved inwards, forming a deep recess that was not visible from the ledge. The ledge canted downwards at an uncomfortable angle, and when I had taken my seat on it, I had my back towards the direction from which I expected the tiger to come, while the tethered buffalo was to my left front, and distant about thirty yards from me.

The sun had set when the buffalo, who had been lying down, scrambled to his feet and faced up the ravine, and a moment later a stone came rolling down. It would not have been possible for me to have fired in the direction from which the sound had come, so to avoid detection I sat perfectly still. After some time the buffalo gradually turned to the left until he was facing in my direction. This showed that whatever he was frightened of – and I could see he was frightened – was in the recess below me. Presently the head of a tiger appeared directly under me. A head-shot at a tiger is only justified in an emergency, and any movement on my part might have betrayed my presence. For a long minute or two the head remained perfectly still, and then, with a quick dash forward, and one great bound, the tiger was on the buffalo. The buffalo, as I have stated, was facing the tiger, and to avoid a frontal attack with the possibility of injury from the buffalo's horns, the tiger's dash carried him to the left of the buffalo, and he made his attack at right angles. There was no fumbling for tooth-hold, no struggle, and no sound beyond the impact of the two heavy bodies, after which the buffalo lay quite still with the tiger lying partly over it and holding it by the throat. It is generally believed that tigers kill by delivering a smashing blow on the neck. This is incorrect. Tigers kill with their teeth.

The right side of the tiger was towards me and, taking careful aim with the .275 I had armed myself with when leaving camp that morning, I fired. Relinquishing its hold on the buffalo, the tiger, without making a sound, turned and bounded off up the ravine and out of sight. Clearly a miss, for which I was unable to assign any reason. If the tiger had not seen me or the flash of the rifle there was a possibility that it would return; so recharging the rifle I sat on.

The buffalo, after the tiger left him, lay without movement, and the conviction grew on me that I had shot him instead of the tiger. Ten, fifteen minutes had dragged by, when the tiger's head for a second time appeared from the recess below me. Again there was a long pause, and then, very slowly, the tiger emerged, walked up to the buffalo and stood looking down at it. With the whole length of the back as a target I was going to make no mistake the second time. Very carefully the sights were aligned, and the trigger slowly pressed; but instead of the tiger's falling dead as I expected it to, it sprang to the left and went tearing up a little side ravine, dislodging stones as it went up the steep hill-side.

Two shots fired in comparatively good light at a range of thirty yards, and heard by anxious villagers for miles round: and all I should have to show for them would be, certainly one, and quite possibly two, bullet holes in a dead buffalo. Clearly my eyesight was failing, or in climbing the rock I had knocked the foresight out of alignment. But on focussing my eyes on small objects I found there was nothing wrong with my eyesight, and a glance along the barrel showed that the sights were all right, so the only reason I could assign for having missed the tiger twice was bad shooting.

There was no chance of the tiger's returning a third time; and even if it did return, there was nothing to be gained by risking the possibility of only wounding it in bad light when I had not been able to kill it while the light had been comparatively good. Under these circumstances there was no object in my remaining any longer on the ledge.

My clothes were still damp from my exertions earlier in the day, a cold wind was blowing and promised to get colder, my shorts were of thin khaki and the rock was hard and cold, and a hot cup of tea awaited me in the village. Good as these reasons were, there was a better and a more convincing reason for my remaining where I was – the man-eater. It was now quite dark. A quarter-of-a-mile walk along a boulder-strewn ravine and a winding path through dense undergrowth lay between me and the village. Beyond the suspicions of the villagers that the tiger they had seen the previous day – and that I had quite evidently just fired at – was the man-eater, I had no definite knowledge of the man-eater's whereabouts; and though at that moment she might have been fifty miles away, she might also have been watching me from a distance of fifty yards; so, uncomfortable as my perch was, prudence dictated that I should remain where I was. As the long hours dragged by, the conviction grew on me that man-eater shooting, by night, was not a pastime that appealed to me, and that if this animal could not be shot during daylight hours she would have to be left to die of old age. This conviction was strengthened when, cold and stiff, I started to climb down as soon as there was sufficient light to shoot by, and slipping on the dew-drenched rock completed the descent with my feet in the air. Fortunately I landed on a bed of sand, without doing myself or the rifle any injury.

Early as it was I found the village astir, and I was quickly the middle of a small crowd. In reply to the eager questions from all sides, I was only able to say that I had been firing at an imaginary tiger with blank ammunition.

A pot of tea drunk while sitting near a roaring fire did much to restore warmth to my inner and outer man, and then, accompanied by most of the men and all the boys of the village, I went to where a rock jutted out over the ravine and directly above my overnight exploit. To the assembled throng I explained how the tiger had appeared from the recess under me and had bounded on to the buffalo, and how, alter I had fired, it had dashed off in that direction; and as I pointed up the ravine there was an excited shout of 'Look, sahib, there's the tiger lying dead!' My eyes were strained with an all-night vigil, but even after looking away and back again there was no denying the fact that the tiger was lying there, dead. To the very natural question of why I had fired a second shot after a period of twenty or thirty minutes, I said that the tiger had appeared a second time from exactly the same place, and that I had fired at it while it was standing near the buffalo, and that it had gone up that side ravine – and there were renewed shouts, in which the women and girls who had now come up joined, of

'Look, sahib, there is another tiger lying dead!' Both tigers appeared to be about the same size, and both were lying sixty yards from where I had fired.

Questioned on the subject of this second tiger, the villagers said that when the four human beings had been killed, and also on the previous day when the bullock had been killed, only one tiger had been seen. The mating season for tigers is an elastic one extending from November to April, and the man-eater – if either of the two tigers lying within view was the man-eater – had evidently provided herself with a mate.

A way into the ravine, down the steep rock face, was found some two hundred yards below where I had sat up, and, followed by the entire population of the village, I went past the dead buffalo to where the first tiger was lying. As I approached it hopes rose high, for she was an old tigress. Handing the rifle to the nearest man I got down on my knees to examine her feet. On that day when the tigress had tried to stalk the women cutting wheat she had left some beautiful pug-marks on the edge of the field. They were the first pug-marks I had seen of the man-eater, and I had examined them very carefully. They showed the tigress to be a very old animal, whose feet had splayed out with age. The pads of the forefeet were heavily rutted, one deep rut running right across the pad of the right forefoot, and the toes were elongated to a length I had never before seen in a tiger. With these distinctive feet it would have been easy to pick the man-eater out of a hundred dead tigers. The animal before me was, I found to my great regret, not the man-eater. When I conveyed this information to the assembled throng of people there was a murmur of strong dissent from all sides. It was asserted that I myself, on my previous visit, had declared the man-eater to be an old tigress, and such an animal I had now shot a few yards from where, only a short time previously, four of their number had been killed. Against this convincing evidence, of what value was the evidence of the feet, for the feet of all tigers were alike!

The second tiger could, under the circumstances, only be a male, and while I made preparations to skin the tigress I sent a party of men to fetch him. The side ravine was steep and narrow, and after a great deal of shouting and laughter the second tiger – a fine male – was laid down alongside the tigress.

The skinning of those two tigers, that had been dead fourteen hours, with the sun beating down on my back and an ever-growing crowd pressing round, was one of the most unpleasant tasks I have ever undertaken. By early afternoon the job was completed, and with the skins neatly tied up for my men to carry I was ready to start on my five-mile walk back to camp.

During the morning, Headmen and others had come in from adjoining villages, and before leaving I assured them that the Chowgarh man-eater was not dead and warned them that the slackening of precautions would give the tigress the opportunity she was waiting for. Had my warning been heeded, the man-eater would not have claimed as many victims as she did during the succeeding months.

There was no further news of the man-eater, and after a stay of a few weeks at Dalkania, I left to keep an appointment with the district officials in the terai.

III

In March 1930 Vivian, our District Commissioner, was touring through the man-eater's domain, and on the 22nd of the month I received an urgent request from him to go to Kala Agar, where he said he would await my arrival. It is roughly fifty miles from Naini Tal to Kala Agar, and two days after receipt of Vivian's letter I arrived in time for breakfast at the Kala Agar Forest Bungalow, where he and Mrs Vivian were staying.

Over breakfast the Vivians told me they had arrived at the bungalow on the afternoon of the 21st, and while they were having tea on the veranda, one of six women who were cutting grass in the compound of the bungalow had been killed and carried off by the man-eater. Rifles were hurriedly seized and, accompanied by some of his staff, Vivian followed up the 'drag' and found the dead woman tucked away under a bush at the foot of an oak-tree. On examining the ground later, I found that on the approach of Vivian's party the tigress had gone off down the hill, and throughout the subsequent proceedings had remained in a thicket of raspberry bushes, fifty yards from the kill. A machan was put up in the oak-tree for Vivian, and two others in trees near the forest road which passed thirty yards above the kill, for members of his staff. The machans were occupied as soon as they were ready, and the party sat up the whole night, without, however, seeing anything of the tigress.

Next morning the body of the woman was removed for cremation, and a young buffalo was tied up on the forest road about half a mile from the bungalow, and killed by the tigress the same night. The following evening the Vivians sat up over the buffalo. There was no moon, and just as daylight was fading out and nearby objects were becoming indistinct, they first heard and then saw an animal coming up to the kill, which in the uncertain light they mistook for a bear; but for this unfortunate mistake their very sporting effort would have resulted in their bagging the man-cater, for both the Vivians are good rifle shots.

On the 25th the Vivians left Kala Agar, and during the course of the day my four buffaloes arrived from Dalkania. As the tigress now appeared to be inclined to accept this form of bait I tied them up at intervals of a few hundred yards along the forest road. For three nights in succession the tigress passed within a few feet of the buffaloes without touching them, but on the fourth night the buffalo nearest the bungalow was killed. On examining the kill in the morning I was disappointed to find that the buffalo had been killed by a pair of leopards I had heard calling the previous night above the bungalow. I did not like the idea of firing in this locality, for fear of" driving away the tigress, but it was quite evident that if I did not shoot the leopards they would kill my three remaining buffaloes, so I stalked them while they were sunning themselves on some big rocks above the kill, and shot both of them.

The forest road from the Kala Agar bungalow runs tor several miles due west through very beautiful forests of pine, oak, and rhododendron, and in thee forests there is, compared with the rest of Kumaon, quite a lot of game in the way of sambur, kakar, and pig, in addition to a great wealth of bird life. On two occasions I suspected the tigress of having killed sambur in this forest, and though on both occasions I found the blood-stained spot where the animal had been killed, I failed to find either of the kills.

For the next fourteen days I spent all the daylight hours either on the forest road, on which no one but myself ever set foot, or in the jungle, and only twice during that period did I get near the tigress. On the first occasion I had been

down to visit an isolated village, on the south face of Kala Agar ridge, that had been abandoned the previous year owing to the depredations of the man-eater, and on the way back had taken a cattle-track that went over the ridge and down the far side to the forest road, when, approaching a pile of rocks, I suddenly felt there was danger ahead. The distance from the ridge to the forest road was roughly three hundred yards. The track, after leaving the ridge, went steeply down for a few yards and then turned to the right and ran diagonally across the hill for a hundred yards; the pile of rocks was about midway on the right-hand side of this length of the track. Beyond the rocks a hairpin bend carried the track to the left, and a hundred yards farther on another sharp bend took it down to its junction with the forest road.

I had been along this track many times, and this was the first occasion on which I hesitated to pass the rocks. To avoid them I should either have had to go several hundred yards through dense undergrowth or make a wide detour round and above them; the former would have subjected me to very great danger, and there was no time for the latter, for the sun was near setting and I had still two miles to go. So, whether I liked it or not, there was nothing for it but to face the rocks. The wind was blowing up the hill, so I was able to ignore the thick cover on the left of the track and concentrate all my attention on the rocks to my right. A hundred feet would see me clear of the danger zone, and this distance I covered foot by foot, walking sideways with my face to the rocks and the rifle to my shoulder; a strange mode of progression, had there been any to see it.

Thirty yards beyond the rocks was an open glade, starting from the right-hand side of the track and extending up the hill for fifty or sixty yards, and screened from the rocks by a fringe of bushes. In this glade a kakar was grazing. I saw her before she saw me, and watched her out of the corner of my eye. On catching sight of me she threw up her head, and as I was not looking in her direction and was moving slowly on she stood stock still, as these animals have a habit of doing when they are under the impression that they have not been seen. On arrival at the hairpin bend I looked over my shoulder and saw that the kakar had lowered her head, and was once more cropping the grass.

I had walked a short distance along the track after passing the bend when the kakar went dashing up the hill, barking hysterically. In a few quick strides I was back at the bend, and was just in time to see a movement in the bushes on the lower side of the track. That the kakar had seen the tigress was quite evident, and the only place where she could have seen her was on the track. The movement I had seen might have been caused by the passage of a bird; on the other hand, it might have been caused by the tigress; anyway, a little investigation was necessary before proceeding farther on my way.

A trickle of water seeping out from under the rocks had damped the red clay of which the track was composed, making an ideal surface for the impression of tracks. In this damp clay I had left footprints, and over these foot-prints I now found the splayed-out pug-marks of the tigress where she had jumped down from the rocks and followed me, until the kakar had seen her and given its alarm-call, whereon the tigress had left the track and entered the bushes where I had seen the movement. The tigress was undoubtedly familiar with every foot of the ground, and not having had an opportunity of killing me at the rocks – and her chance of bagging me at the first hairpin bend having been spoilt by the kakar – she was probably now making her way through the dense under-growth to try to intercept me at the second bend.

Further progress along the track was now not advisable, so I followed the kakar up the glade, and turning to the left, worked my way down, over open ground, to the forest road below. Had there been sufficient daylight I believe I could, that evening, have turned the tables on the tigress, for the conditions, after she left the shelter of the rocks, were all in my favour. I knew the ground as well as she did, and while she had no reason to suspect my intentions towards her, I had the advantage of knowing, very clearly, her intentions towards me. However, though the conditions were in my favour, I was unable to take advantage of them owing to the lateness of the evening.

I have made mention elsewhere of the sense that warns us of impending danger, and will not labour the subject further beyond stating that this sense is a very real one and that I do not know, and therefore cannot explain, what brings it into operation. On this occasion I had neither heard nor seen the tigress, nor had I received any indication from bird or beast of her presence, and yet I knew, without any shadow of doubt, that she was lying up for me among the rocks. I had been out for many hours that day and had covered many miles of jungle with unflagging caution, but without one moment's unease, and then, on cresting the ridge and coming in sight of the rocks, I knew they held danger for me, and this knowledge was confirmed a few minutes later by the kakar's warning call to the jungle folk, and by my finding the man-eater's pug-marks superimposed on my footprints.

IV

To those of my readers who have had the patience to accompany me so far in my narrative, I should like to give a clear and a detailed account of my first – and last – meeting with the tigress.

The meeting took place in the early afternoon of 11 April 1930, nineteen days after my arrival at Kala Agar.

I had gone out that day at 2 p.m. with the intention of tying up my three buffaloes at selected places along the forest road, when at a point a mile from the bungalow, where the road crosses a ridge and goes from the north to the west face of the Kala Agar range, I came on a large party of men who had been out collecting firewood. In the party was an old man who, pointing down the hill to a thicket of young oak-trees some five hundred yards from where we were standing, said it was in that thicket where the man-eater, a month previously, had killed his only son, a lad eighteen years of age. I had not heard the father's version of the killing of his son, so, while we sat on the edge of the road smoking, he told his story, pointing out the spot where the lad had been killed, and where all that was left of him had been found the following day. The old man blamed the twenty-five men who had been out collecting firewood on that day for the death of his son, saying, very bitterly, that they had run away and left him to be killed by the tiger. Some of the men sitting near me had been in that party of twenty-five, and they hotly repudiated responsibility for the lad's death, accusing him of having been responsible for the stampede by screaming out that he had heard the tiger growling and telling everyone to run for their lives. This did not satisfy the old man. He shook his head and said, 'You are grown men and he was only a boy, and you ran away and left him to be killed.' I was sorry for having asked the questions that had led to this heated discussion, and more to placate the old man than for any good it would do, I said I would tie up one of my buffaloes near the spot where he said his son had been killed. So, handing two of the buffaloes over to the party to take back to the bungalow, I set off followed by two of my men leading the remaining buffalo.

A footpath, taking off close to where we had been sitting, went down the hill to the valley below and zigzagged up the opposite pine-clad slope to join the forest road two miles farther on. The path passed close to an open patch of ground which bordered the oak-thicket in which the lad had been killed. On this patch of ground, which was about thirty yards square, there was a solitary pine-sapling. This I cut down. I tied the buffalo to the stump, set one man to cutting a supply of grass for it, and sent the other man, Madho Singh, who served in the Garhwalis during the Great War and is now serving in the United Provinces Civil Pioneer Force, up an oak-tree with instructions to strike a dry branch with the head of his axe and call at the top of his voice as hill people do when cutting leaves for their cattle. I then took up a position on a rock, about four feet high, on the lower edge of the open ground. Beyond the rock the hill fell steeply away to the valley below and was densely clothed with tree and scrub jungle.

The man on the ground had made several trips with the grass he had cut, and Madho Singh on the tree was alternately shouting and singing lustily, while I stood on the rock smoking, with the rifle in the hollow of my left arm, when, all at once, I became aware that the man-eater had arrived. Beckoning urgently to the man on the ground to come to me, I whistled to attract Madho Singh's attention and signalled to him to remain quiet. The ground on three sides was comparatively open. Madho Singh on the tree was to my left front, the man cutting grass had been in front of me, while the buffalo – now showing signs of uneasiness – was to my right front. In this area the tigress could not have approached without my seeing her; and as she *had* approached, there was only one place where she could now be, and that was behind and immediately below me.

When taking up my position I had noticed that the farther side of the rock was steep and smooth, that it extended down the hill for eight or ten feet, and that the lower portion of it was masked by thick undergrowth and young pine-saplings. It would have been a little difficult, but quite possible, for the tigress to have climbed the rock, and I relied for my safety on hearing her in the under-growth should she make the attempt.

I have no doubt that the tigress, attracted, as I had intended she should be, by the noise Madho Singh was making, had come to the rock, and that it was while she was looking up at me and planning her next move that I had become aware of her presence. My change of front, coupled with the silence of the men, may have made her suspicious; anyway, after a lapse of a few minutes, I heard a dry twig snap a little way down the hill; thereafter the feeling of unease left me, and the tension relaxed. An opportunity lost; but there was still a very good chance of my getting a shot, for she would undoubtedly return before long, and when she found us gone would probably content herself with killing the buffalo. There were still four or five hours of daylight, and by crossing the valley and going up the opposite slope I should be able to overlook the whole of the hill-side on which the buffalo was tethered. The shot, if I did get one, would be a long one of from two to three hundred yards, but the .275 rifle I was carrying was accurate, and even if I only wounded the tigress I should have a blood trail to follow, which would be better than feeling about for her in hundreds of square miles of jungle, as I had been doing these many months.

The men were a difficulty. To have sent them back to the bungalow alone would have been nothing short of murder, so of necessity I kept them with me.

Tying the buffalo to the stump in such a manner as to make it impossible for the tigress to carry it away, I left the open ground and rejoined the path to carry out the plan I have outlined, of trying to get a shot from the opposite hill.

About a hundred yards along the path I came to a ravine. On the far side of this, the path entered very heavy undergrowth, and as it was inadvisable to go into thick cover with two men following me, I decided to take to the ravine, follow it down to its junction with the valley, work up the valley, and pick up the path on the far side of the undergrowth.

The ravine was about ten yards wide and four or five feet deep, and as I stepped down into it a nightjar fluttered off a rock on which I had put my hand. On looking at the spot from which the bird had risen, I saw two eggs. These eggs, straw-coloured, with rich brown markings, were of a most unusual shape, one being long and very pointed, while the other was as round as a marble; and as my collection lacked nightjar eggs I decided to add this odd clutch to it. I had no receptacle of any kind in which to carry the eggs, so cupping my left hand I placed the eggs in it and packed them round with a little moss.

As I went down the ravine the banks became higher, and sixty yards from where I had entered it I came on a deep drop of some twelve to fourteen feet. The water that rushes down all these hill ravines in the rains had worn the rock as smooth as glass, and as it was too steep to offer a foot-hold I handed the rifle to the men and, sitting on the edge, proceeded to slide down. My feet had hardly touched the sandy bottom when the two men, with a flying leap, landed one on either side of me, and thrusting the rifle into my hand asked in a very agitated manner if I had heard the tiger. As a matter of fact I had heard nothing, possibly due to the scraping of my clothes on the rocks, and when questioned, the men said that what they had heard was a deep-throated growl from somewhere close at hand, but exactly from which direction the sound had come, they were unable to say. Tigers do not betray their presence by growling when looking for their dinner, and the only, and very unsatisfactory, explanation I can offer is that the tigress followed us after we left the open ground, and on seeing that we were going down the ravine had gone ahead and taken up a position where the ravine narrowed to half its width; and that when she was on the point of springing out on me, I had disappeared out of sight down the slide and she had involuntarily given vent to her disappointment with a low growl. Not a satisfactory reason, unless one assumes – without any reason – that she had selected me for her dinner, and therefore had no interest in the two men.

Where the three of us now stood in a bunch we had the smooth steep rock behind us, to our right a wall of rock slightly leaning over the ravine and fifteen feet high, and to our left a tumbled bank of big rocks thirty or forty feet high. The sandy bed of the ravine, on which we were standing, was roughly forty feet long and ten feet wide. At the lower end of this sandy bed a great pine-tree had fallen across, damming the ravine, and the collection of sand was due to this dam. The wall of overhanging rock came to an end twelve or fifteen feet from the fallen tree, and as I approached the end of the rock, my feet making no sound on the sand, I very fortunately noticed that the sandy bed continued round to the back of the rock.

This rock about which I have said so much I can best describe as a giant school slate, two feet thick at its lower end, and standing up – not quite perpendicularly – on one of its long sides.

As I stepped clear of this giant slate, I looked behind me over my right shoulder and – looked straight into the tigress's face.

I would like you to have a clear picture of the situation.

The sandy bed behind the rock was quite fiat. To the right of it was the smooth slate fifteen feet high and leaning slightly outwards, to the left of it was a scoured-out steep bank also some fifteen feet high overhung by a dense tangle of thorn bushes, while at the far end was a slide similar to, but a little higher than, the one I had glissaded down. The sandy bed, enclosed by these three natural walls, was about twenty feet long and half as wide, and lying on it, with her fore-paws stretched out and her hind legs well tucked under her, was the tigress. Her head, which was raised a few inches off her paws, was eight feet (measured later) from me, and on her face was a smile, similar to that one sees on the face of a dog welcoming his master home after a long absence.

Two thoughts flashed through my mind: one, that it was up to me to make the first move, and the other, that the move would have to be made in such a manner as not to alarm the tigress or make her nervous.

The rifle was in my right hand held diagonally across my chest, with the safety-catch off, and in order to get it to bear on the tigress the muzzle would have to be swung round three-quarters of a circle.

The movement of swinging round the rifle, with one hand, was begun very slowly, and hardly perceptibly, and when a quarter of a circle had been made, the stock came in contact with my right side. It was now necessary to extend my arm, and as the stock cleared my side, the swing was very slowly continued. My arm was now at full stretch and the weight of the rifle was beginning to tell. Only a little farther now for the muzzle to go, and the tigress – who had not once taken her eyes off mine – was still looking up at me, with the pleased expression still on her face.

How long it took the rifle to make the three-quarter circle, I am not in a position to say. To me, looking into the tigress's eyes and unable therefore to follow the movement of the barrel, it appeared that my arm was paralysed, and that the swing would never be completed. However, the movement was completed at last, and as soon as the rifle was pointing at the tiger's body, I pressed the trigger.

I heard the report, exaggerated in that restricted space, and felt the jar of the recoil, and but for these tangible proofs that the rifle had gone off, I might, for all the immediate result the shot produced, have been in the grip of one of those awful nightmares in which triggers are vainly pulled of rifles that refuse to be discharged at the critical moment.

For a perceptible fraction of time the tigress remained perfectly still, and then, very slowly, her head sank on to her outstretched paws, while at the same time a jet of blood issued from the bullet-hole. The bullet had injured her spine and shattered the upper portion of her heart.

The two men who were following a few yards behind me, and who were separated from the tigress by the thickness of the rock, came to a halt when they saw me stop and turn my head. They knew instinctively that I had seen the tigress and judged from my behaviour that she was close at hand, and Madho Singh said afterwards that he wanted to call out and tell me to drop the eggs and get both hands on the rifle. When I had fired my shot and lowered the point of the rifle on to my toes, Madho Singh, at a sign, came forward to relieve me of it, for very suddenly my legs appeared to be unable to support me, so I made for the fallen tree and sat down. Even before looking at the pads of her feet I knew it was the Chowgarh tigress I had sent to the Happy Hunting Grounds, and that the shears that had assisted her to cut the threads of sixty-four human lives – the people of the district put the number at twice that figure – had, while the game was in her hands, turned, and cut the thread of her own life.

Three things, each of which would appear to you to have been to my disadvantage, were actually in my favour. These were: (a) the eggs in my left hand, (b) the light rifle I was carrying, and (c) the tiger being a man-eater. If I had not had the eggs in my hand I should have had both hands on the rifle, and when I looked back and saw the tiger at such close quarters I should instinctively have tried to swing round to face her, and the spring that was arrested by my Jack of movement would inevitably have been launched. Again, if the rifle had not been a light one it would not have been possible for me to have moved it in the way it was imperative I should move it, and then discharge it at the full extent of my arm. And lastly, if the tiger had been just an ordinary tiger, and not a man-eater, it would, on finding itself cornered, have made for the opening and wiped me out of the way; and to be wiped out of the way by a tiger usually has fatal results.

While the men made a detour and went up the hill to free the buffalo and secure the rope, which was needed for another and more pleasant purpose, I climbed over the rocks and wen t up the ravine to restore the eggs to their rightful owner. 1 plead guilty to being as superstitious as my brother sportsmen. For three long periods, extending over a whole year, I had tried – and tried hard – to get a shot at the tigress, and had failed; and now within a few minutes of having picked up the eggs my luck had changed.

The eggs, which all this time had remained safely in the hollow of my left hand, were still warm when I replaced them in the little depression in the rock that did duty as a nest, and when I again passed that way half an hour later, they had vanished under the brooding mother, whose clouring so exactly matched the mottled rock that it was difficult for me, who knew the exact spot where the nest was situated, to distinguish her from her surroundings.

The buffalo, who, after months of care was now so tame that it followed like a dog, came scrambling down the hill in the wake of the men, nosed the tigress, and lay down on the sand to chew the cud of contentment, while we lashed the tigress to the stout pole the men had rut.

I had tried to get Madho Singh to return to the bungalow for help, but this he would not hear of doing. With no one would he and his companion share the honour of carrying in the man-eater, and if I would lend a hand the task, he said, with frequent halts for rest, would not be too difficult. We were three hefty men – two accustomed from childhood to carrying heavy loads – and all three hardened by a life of exposure; but even so, the task we set ourselves was a herculean one.

The path down which we had come was too narrow and too winding for the long pole to which the tigress was lashed, so, with frequent halts to regain breath and re-adjust pads to prevent the pole biting too deep into shoulder muscles, we went straight up the hill through a tangle of raspberry and briar bushes, on the thorns of which we left a portion of our clothing and an amount of skin which made bathing for many days a painful operation.

The sun was still shining on the surrounding hills when three dishevelled and very happy men, followed by a buffalo, carried the tigress to the Kala Agar Forest Bungalow, and from that evening to this day no human being has been killed – or wounded – over the hundreds of square miles of mountain and vale over which the Chowgarh tigress, for a period of five years, held sway.

I have added one more cross and date to the map of Eastern Kumaon that hangs on the wall before me – the cross and the date the man-eater earned. The cross is two miles west of Kala Agar, and the date under it is 11 April 1930.

The tigress's claws were broken and bushed out, and one of her canine teeth was broken, and her front teeth were worn down to the bone. It was these defects that had made her a man-eater and were the cause of her not being able to kill outright – and by her own efforts – a large proportion of the human beings she had attacked since the day she had been deprived of the assistance of the cub I had, on my first visit, shot by mistake.

THE BACHELOR OF POWALGARH

Three miles from our winter home, and in the heart of the forest, there is an open glade some four hundred yards long and half as wide, grassed with emerald-green and surrounded with big trees interlaced with cane creepers. It was in this glade, which for beauty has no equal, that I first saw the tiger who was known throughout the United Provinces as 'The Bachelor of Powalgarh', who from 1920 to 1930 was the most sought-after big-game trophy in the province.

The sun had just risen, one winter's morning, when I crested the high ground overlooking the glade. On the far side, a score of red jungle fowl were scratching among the dead leaves bordering a crystal-clear stream, and scattered over the emerald-green grass, now sparkling with dew, fifty or more chital were feeding. Sitting on a tree-stump and smoking, I had been looking at this scene for some time when the hind nearest to me raised her head, turned in my direction, and called; and a moment later the Bachelor stepped into the open, from the thick bushes below me. For a long minute he stood with head held high surveying the scene, and then with slow unhurried steps started to cross the glade. In his rich winter coat, which the newly risen sun was lighting up, he was a magnificent sight as, with head turning now to the right and now to the left, he walked down the wide lane the deer had made for him. At the stream he lay down and quenched his thirst, then sprang across and, as he entered the dense tree jungle beyond, called three times in acknowledgment of the homage the jungle folk had paid him, for from the time he had entered the glade every chital had called, every jungle fowl had cackled, and every one of a troupe of monkeys on the trees had chattered.

The Bachelor was far afield that morning, for his home was in a ravine six miles away. Living in an area in which the majority of tigers are bagged with the aid of elephants, he had chosen his home wisely. The ravine, running into the foot-hills, was half a mile long, with steep hills on either side rising to a height of a thousand feet. At the upper end of the ravine there was a waterfall some twenty feet high, and at the lower end, where the water bad cut through red clay, it narrowed to four feet. Any sportsman, therefore, who wished to try conclusions with the Bachelor, while he was at home, would of a necessity have to do so on foot. It was this secure retreat, and the Government rules prohibiting night shooting, that had enabled the Bachelor to retain possession of his much sought-after skin.

In spite of the many and repeated attempts that had been made to bag him with the aid of buffalo bait, the Bachelor had never been fired at, though on two occasions, to my knowledge, he had only escaped death by the skin of his teeth. On the first occasion, after a perfect beat, a guy rope by which the machan was suspended interfered with the movement of Fred Anderson's rifle at the critical moment, and on the second occasion the Bachelor arrived at the machan before the beat started and found Huish Edye filling his pipe. On both these occasions he had been viewed at a range of only a few feet, and while Anderson described him as being as big as a Shetland pony, Edye said he was as big as a donkey.

The winter following these and other unsuccessful attempts, I took Wyndham, our Commissioner, who knows more about tigers than any other man in India, to a fire-track skirting the upper end of the ravine in which the Bachelor lived, to show him the fresh pug-marks of the tiger which I had found on the fire-track that morning. Wyndham was accompanied by two of his most experienced shikaris, and after the three of them had carefully measured and examined the pug-marks, Wyndham said that in his opinion the tiger was ten feet between pegs, and while one shikari said he was 10 feet 5 inches over curves, the other said he was 10 feet 6 inches or a little more. All three agreed that they had never seen the pug-marks of a bigger tiger.

In 1930 the Forest Department started extensive fellings in the area surrounding the Bachelor's home and, annoyed at the disturbance, he changed his quarters; this I learnt from two sportsmen who had taken out a shooting pass with the object of hunting down the tiger. Shooting passes are only issued for fifteen days of each month, and throughout that winter, shooting party after shooting party failed to make contact with the tiger.

Towards the end of the winter an old dak runner, who passes our gate every morning and evening on his seven-mile run through the forest to a hill village, came to me one evening and reported that on his way out that morning he had seen the biggest pug-marks of a tiger that he had seen during the thirty years of his service. The tiger, he said, had come from the west and, after proceeding along the road for two hundred yards, had gone east, taking a path that started from near an almond-tree. This tree was about two miles from our home, and was a well-known landmark. The path the tiger had taken runs through very heavy jungle for half a mile before crossing a wide watercourse, and then joins a cattle-track which skirts the foot of the hills before entering a deep and well-wooded valley; a favourite haunt of tigers.

Early next morning, with Robin at my heels, I set out to prospect, my objective being the point where the cattle-track entered the valley, for at this point the tracks of all the animals entering or leaving the valley are to be found. From the time we started, Robin appeared to know that we had a special job in hand, and he paid not the least attention to the jungle fowl we disturbed, the kakar (barking deer) that let us get quite close to it, and the two sambur that stood and belled at us. Where the cattle-track entered the valley the ground was hard and stony, and when we reached this spot Robin put down his head and very carefully smelt the stones, and on receiving a signal from me to carry on he turned and started down the track, keeping a yard ahead of me; I could tell from his behaviour that he was on the scent of a tiger, and that the scent was hot. A hundred yards farther down, where the track flattens out and runs along the foot of the hill, the ground is soft; here I saw the pug-marks of a tiger, and a glance at them satisfied me we were on the heels of the Bachelor and that he was only a minute or two ahead of us.

Beyond the soft ground the track runs for three hundred yards over stones, before going steeply down on to an open plain. If the tiger kept to the track we should probably see him on this open ground. We had gone another fifty yards when Robin stopped and, after running his nose up and down a blade of grass on the left of the track, turned and entered the grass, which was here about two feet high. On the far side of the grass there was a patch of clerodendron, about forty yards wide. This plant grows in dense patches to a height of five feet, and has widely spread leaves and a big head of flowers not unlike horse-chestnut. It is greatly fancied by tiger, sambur, and pig because of the shade it gives. When Robin reached the clerodendron he stopped and backed towards me, thus telling me that he could not see into the bushes ahead and wished to be carried. Lifting him up, I put his hind legs into my left-hand pocket, and when he had hooked his forefeet over my left arm, he was safe and secure, and I had both hands free for the rifle. On these occasions Robin was always in deadly earnest, and no matter what he saw, or how our quarry behaved before or after being fired at, he never moved and spoilt my shot, or impeded my view. Proceeding very slowly, we had gone half-way through the clerodendron when I saw the bushes directly in front of us swaying. Waiting until the tiger had cleared the bushes, I went forward expecting to see him in the more or less open jungle, but he was nowhere in sight, and when I put Robin down he turned to the left and indicated that the tiger had gone into a deep and narrow ravine near by. This ravine ran to the foot of an isolated hill on which there were caves frequented by tigers, and as I was not armed to deal with a tiger at close quarters, and further, as it was time for breakfast, Robin and I turned and made for home.

After breakfast I returned alone, armed with a heavy .450 rifle, and as I approached the hill, which in the days of the long ago had been used by the local inhabitants as a rallying point against the Gurkha invaders, I heard the boom of a big buffalo bell, and a man shouting. These sounds were coming from the top of the hill, which is flat, and about half an acre in extent, so I climbed up and saw a man on a tree, striking a dead branch with the head of his axe and shouting, while at the foot of the tree a number of buffaloes were collected. When he saw me the man called out, saying I had just arrived in time to save him and his buffaloes from a shaitan of a tiger, the size of a camel, that had been threatening them for hours. From his story I gathered that he had arrived on the hill shortly after Robin and I had left for home, and that as he started to cut bamboo leaves for his buffaloes he saw a tiger coming towards him. He shouted to drive the tiger away, as he had done on many previous occasions with other tigers, but instead of going away this one had started to growl. He took to his heels, followed by his buffaloes, and climbed up the nearest tree. The tiger, paying no heed to his shouts, had then set to pacing round and round, while the buffaloes kept their heads towards it. Probably the tiger had heard me coming, for it had left only a moment before I had arrived. The man was an old friend, who before his quarrel with the Headman of his village had done a considerable amount of poaching in these jungles with the Headman's gun. He now begged me to conduct both himself and his cattle safely out of the jungle; so telling him to lead on, 1 followed behind to see that there were no stragglers. At first the buffaloes were disinclined to break up their close formation, but after a little persuasion we got them to start, and we had gone half-way across the open plain I have alluded to when the tiger called in the jungle to our right. The man quickened his pace, and I urged on the buffaloes, for a mile of very thick jungle lay between us and the wide, open watercourse beyond which lay my friend's village and safety for his buffaloes.

I have earned the reputation of being keener on photographing animals than on killing them, and before I left my friend he begged me to put aside photography for this once, and kill the tiger, which he said was big enough to eat a buffalo a day, and ruin him in twenty-five days. I promised to do my best and turned to re-trace my steps to the open plain, to meet with an experience every detail of which has burnt itself deep into my memory.

On reaching the plain I sat down to wait for the tiger to disclose his whereabouts, or for the jungle folk to tell me where he was. It was then about 3 p.m., and as the sun was warm and comforting, I put my head down on my drawn-up knees and had been dozing a few minutes when I was awakened by the tiger calling; thereafter he continued to call at short intervals.

Between the plain and the hills there is a belt, some half-mile wide, of the densest scrub jungle for a hundred miles round, and I located the tiger as being on the hills on the far side of the scrub – about three-quarters of a mile from me – and from the way he was calling it was evident he was in search of a mate.

Starting from the upper left-hand corner of the plain, and close to where I was sitting, an old cart-track, used some years previously for extracting timber, ran in an almost direct line to where the tiger was calling. This track would take me in the direction of the calling animal, but on the hills was high grass, and without Robin to help me there would be little chance of my seeing him. So instead of my going to look for the tiger, I decided he should come and look for me. I was too far away for him to hear me, so I sprinted up the cart-track for a few hundred yards, laid down my rifle, climbed to the top of a high tree and called three times. I was immediately answered by the tiger. After climbing down, I ran back, calling as I went, and arrived on the plain without having found a suitable place in which to sit and await the tiger.. Something would have to be done and done in a hurry, for the tiger was rapidly coming nearer; so, after rejecting a little hollow which I found to be full of black stinking water, I lay down flat in the open, twenty yards from where the track entered the scrub. From this point I had a clear view up the track for fifty yards, to where a bush, leaning over it, impeded my farther view. If the tiger came down the track, as I expected him to, I decided to fire at him as soon as he cleared the obstruction.

After opening the rifle to make quite sure it was loaded, I threw off the safety-catch, and with elbows comfortably resting on the soft ground waited for the tiger to appear. I had not called since I came out on the plain, so to give him direction I now gave a low call, which he immediately answered from a distance of a hundred yards. If he came on at his usual pace, I judged he would clear the obstruction in thirty seconds. I counted this number very slowly, and went on counting up to eighty, when out of the corner of my eye I saw a movement to my right front, where the bushes approached to within ten yards of me. Turning my eyes in that direction I saw a great head projecting above the bushes, which here were four feet high. The tiger was only a foot or two inside the bushes, but all I could see of him was his head. As I very slowly swung the point of the rifle round and ran my eyes along the sights I noticed that his head was not quite square on to me, and as I was firing up, and he was looking down I aimed an inch below his right eye, pressed the trigger, and for the next half-hour nearly died of fright.

Instead of dropping dead as I expected him to, the tiger went straight up into the air above the bushes for his full length, falling backwards on to a tree a foot thick which had been blown down in a storm and was still green. With unbelievable fury he attacked this tree and tore it to bits, emitting a5 he did so roar upon roar, and what was even worse, a dreadful blood-curdling sound as though he was savaging his worst enemy. The branches of the tree tossed about as though struck by a tornado, while the bushes on my side shook and bulged out, and every moment I expected to have him on top of me, for he had been looking at me when I fired, and knew where I was.

Too frightened even to re-charge the rifle for fear the slight movement and sound should attract the attention or the tiger, I lay and sweated for half an hour with my finger on the left trigger. At last the branches of the tree and the bushes ceased waving about, and the roaring became less frequent, and eventually, to my great relief, ceased. For another half-hour I lay perfectly still, with arms cramped by the weight of the heavy rifle, and then started to pull myself backwards with my toes. After progressing for thirty yards in this manner I got to my feet, and, crouching low, made for the welcome shelter of the nearest tree. Here I remained for some minutes, and as all was now silent I turned and made for home.

T1

Next morning I returned accompanied by one of my men, an expert tree-climber. I had noticed the previous evening that there was a tree growing on the edge or the open ground, and about forty yards from where the tiger had fallen. We approached this tree very cautiously, and I stood behind it while the man climbed to the top. After a long and a careful scrutiny he looked down and shook his head, and when he re-joined me on the ground he told me that the bushes over a big area had been flattened down, but that the tiger was not in sight.

I sent him back to his perch on the tree with instructions to keep a sharp look-oat and warn me if he saw any movement in the bushes, and went forward to have a look at the spot where the tiger had raged. He had raged to some purpose, for, in addition to tearing branches and great strips of wood off the tree, he had torn up several bushes by the roots, and bitten down others. Blood in profusion was sprinkled everywhere, and on the ground were two congealed pools, near one of which was lying a bit of bone two inches square, which I found on examination to be part of the tiger's skull.

No blood trail led away from this spot, and this, combined with the two pools of blood, was proof that the tiger was still here when I left and that the precautions I had taken the previous evening had been very necessary, for when I started on my 'get-away' I was only ten yards from the most dangerous animal in the world – a freshly wounded tiger. On circling round the spot I found a small smear of blood here and there on leaves that had brushed against his face. Noting that these indications of the tiger's passage led in a direct line to a giant semul-trce two hundred yards away, I went back and climbed the tree my man was on in order to get a bird's-eye view of the ground I should have to go over, for I had a very uneasy feeling that I should find him alive: a tiger shot in the head can live for days, and can even recover from the wound. True, this tiger had a bit of his skull missing, and as I had never dealt with an animal in his condition before I did not know whether he was likely to live for a few hours or days, or live on to die of old age. For this reason I decided to treat him as an ordinary wounded tiger, and not to take any avoidable risk when following him up.

From my elevated position on the tree I saw that, a little to the left of the line to the semul-tree, there were two trees, the nearer one thirty yards from where the blood was, and the other fifty yards farther on. Leaving my man on the tree, I climbed down, picked up my rifle and a shot-gun and bag of a hundred cartridges, and very cautiously approached the nearer tree and climbed up it to a height of thirty feet, pulling the rifle and gun which I had tied to one end of a strong cord, up after me. After fixing the rifle in a fork of the tree where it would be handy if needed, I started to spray the bushes with small shot, yard by yard up to the foot of the second tree. I did this with the object of locating the tiger, assuming he was alive and in that area, for a wounded tiger, on hearing a shot fired close to him, or on being struck by a pellet, will either growl or charge. Receiving no indication of the tiger's presence I went to the second tree, and sprayed the bushes to within a few yards of the semul-tree, firing the last shot at the tree itself. After this last shot 1 thought I heard a low growl, but it was not repeated, and I put it down to my imagination. My bag of cartridges was now empty, so after recovering my man I called it a day, and went home.

When I returned next morning I found my friend the buffalo man feeding his buffaloes on the plain. He appeared to be very much relieved to see me, and the reason for this I learnt later. The grass was still wet with dew, but we found a dry spot and there sat down to have a smoke and relate our experiences. My friend, as I have already told you, had done a lot of poaching, and having spent all his life in tiger-infested jungles tending his buffaloes, or shooting, his jungle knowledge was considerable.

After I had left him that day at the wide, open watercourse, he had crossed to the far side and had sat down to listen for sounds coming from the direction in which I had gone. He had heard two tigers calling; he had heard my shot followed by the continuous roaring of a tiger, and very naturally concluded that I had wounded one of the tigers and that it had killed me. On his return next morning to the same spot, he had been greatly mystified by hearing a hundred shots fired, and this morning, not being able to contain his curiosity any longer, he had come to see what had happened. Attracted by the smell of blood, his buffaloes had shown him where the tiger had fallen, and he had seen the patches of dry blood and had found the bit of bone. No animal in his opinion could possibly live for more than a few hours after having a bit of its skull blown away, and so sure was he that the tiger was dead that he offered to take his buffaloes into the jungle and find it for me. I had heard of this method of recovering tigers with the help of buffaloes, but had never tried it myself, and after my friend had agreed to accepting compensation for any damage to his cattle I accepted his offer.

Rounding up the buffaloes, twenty-five in number, and keeping to the line I had sprinkled with shot the previous day, we made for the semul-trce, followed by the buffaloes, Our progress was slow, for not only had we to move the chin-high bushes with our hands to see where to put our feet, but we also had frequently to check a very natural tendency on the part of the buffaloes to stray. As we approached the semul-trce, where the bushes were lighter, I saw a little hollow filled with dead leaves that had been pressed flat and on which were several patches of blood, some dry, others in process of congealing, and one quite fresh; and when I put my hand to the ground I found it was warm. Incredible as it may appear, the tiger had lain in this hollow the previous day while I had expended a hundred cartridges, and had only moved off when he saw us and the buffaloes approaching. The buffaloes had now found the blood and were pawing up the ground and snorting, and, as the prospect of being caught between a charging tiger and angry buffaloes did not appeal to me, I took hold of my friend's arm, turned him round, and made for the open plain, followed by the buffaloes. When we were back on safe ground I told the man to go home, and said I would return next day and deal with the tiger alone.

The path through the jungles that I had taken each day when coming from and going home ran for some distance over soft ground, and on this soft ground, on this fourth day, I found the pug-marks of a big male tiger. By following these pug-marks I found the tiger had entered the dense brushwood a hundred yards to the right of the semul-tree. Here was an unexpected complication, for if I now saw a tiger in this jungle I should not know – unless I got very a close look at it – whether it was the wounded or the unwounded one. However, this contingency would have to be dealt with when met, and in the meantime worrying would not help, so I entered the bushes and made for the hollow at the foot of the semul-tree.

There was no blood trail to follow, so I zigzagged through the bushes, into which it was impossible to see farther than a few inches, for an hour or more, until I came to a ten-foot-wide dry watercourse. Before stepping down into this watercourse I looked up it, and saw the left hind leg and tail of a tiger. The tiger was standing perfectly still with its body and head hidden by a tree, and only this one leg visible. I raised the rifle to my shoulder, and then lowered it. To have broken the leg would have been easy, for the tiger was only ten yards away, and it would have been the right thing to do if its owner was the wounded animal; but there were two tigers in this area, and to have broken the leg of the wrong one would have doubled my difficulties, which were already considerable. Presently the leg was withdrawn and I heard the tiger moving away, and going to the spot where he had been standing I found a few drops of blood – too late now to regret not having broken that leg.

A quarter of a mile farther on there was a little stream, and it was possible that the tiger, now recovering from his wound, was making for this stream. With the object of intercepting him, or failing that, waiting for him at the water, I took a game-path which I knew went to the stream and had proceeded along it for some distance when a sambur belled to my left, and went dashing off through the jungle. It was evident now that I was abreast of the tiger, and I had only taken a few more steps when I heard the loud crack of a dry stick breaking as though some heavy animal had fallen on it; the sound had come from a distance of fifty yards and from the exact spot where the sambur had belled. The sambur had in unmistakable tones warned the jungle folk of the presence of a tiger, and the stick therefore could only have been broken by the same animal; so getting down on my hands and knees I started to crawl in the direction from which the sound had come.

The bushes here were from six to eight feet high, with dense foliage on the upper branches and very few leaves on the stems, so that I could see through them for a distance of ten to fifteen feet. I had covered thirty yards, hoping fervently that if the tiger charged he would come from in front (for in no other direction could I have fired), when I caught sight of something red on which the sun, drifting through the upper leaves, was shining; it might only be a bunch of dead leaves; on the other hand, it might be the tiger. I could get a better view of this object from two yards to the right, so, lowering my head until my chin touched the ground, I crawled this distance with belly to ground, and on raising my head saw the tiger in front of me. He was crouching down looking at me, with the sun shining on his left shoulder, and on receiving my two bullets he rolled over on his side without making a sound.

As I stood over him and ran my eyes over his magnificent proportions it was not necessary to examine the pads of his feet to know that before me lay the Bachelor of Powalgarh.

The entry of the bullet fired four days previously was hidden by a wrinkle of skin, and at the back of his head was a big hole which, surprisingly, was perfectly clean and healthy.

The report of my rifle was, I knew, being listened for, so I hurried home to relieve anxiety, and while I related the last chapter of the hunt and drank a pot of tea, my men were collecting.

Accompanied by my sister and Robin and a carrying party of twenty men, I returned to where the tiger was lying, and before he was roped to a pole my sister and I measured him from nose to tip of tail, and from tip of tail to nose. At home we again measured him to make quite sure we had made no mistake the first time. These measurements are valueless, for there were no independent witnesses present to certify them; they are, however, interesting as showing the accuracy with which experienced woodsmen can judge the length of a tiger from his pug-marks. Wyndham, you will remember, said the tiger was ten feet between pegs, which would roughly give 10 feet 6 inches over curves; and while one shikari said he was 10 feet 5 inches over curves, the other said he was IO feet 6 inches or a little more. Shot seven years after these estimates were made, my sister and I measured the tiger as being 10 feet 7 inches over curves.

I have told the story at some length, as I feel sure that those who hunted the tiger between 1920 and 1930 will be interested to know how the Bachelor of Powalgarh met his end.

THE MOHAN MAN-EATER

Eighteen miles from our summer home in the Himalayas there is a long ridge running east and west, some 9,000 feet in height. On the upper slopes of the eastern end of this ridge there is a luxuriant growth of oat-grass; below this grass the hill falls steeply away in a series of rock cliffs to the Kosi River below.

One day a party of women and girls from the village on the north face of the ridge were cutting the oat-grass, when a tiger suddenly appeared in their midst. In the stampede that followed an elderly woman lost her footing, rolled down the steep slope, and disappeared over the cliff. The tiger, evidently alarmed by the screams of the women, vanished as mysteriously as it had appeared, and when the women had re-assembled and recovered from their fright, they went down the grassy slope and, looking over the cliff, saw their companion lying on a narrow ledge some distance below them.

The woman said she was badly injured – it was found later that she had broken a leg and fractured several ribs – and that she could not move. Ways and means of a rescue were discussed, and it was finally decided that it was a job for men; and as no one appeared to be willing to remain at the spot, they informed the injured woman that they were going back to the village for help. The woman begged not to be left alone, however, and at her entreaty a girl, sixteen years of age, volunteered to stay with her. So, while the rest of the party set off for the village, the girl made her way down to the right, where a rift in the cliff enabled her to get a foothold on the ledge.

This ledge extended only half-way across the face of the cliff and ended, a few yards from where the woman was lying, in a shallow depression. Fearing that she might fall off the ledge and be killed on the rocks hundreds of feet below, the woman asked the girl to move her to this depression, and this difficult and dangerous feat the girl successfully accomplished. There was only room for one in the depression, so the girl squatted, as only an Indian can squat, on the ledge facing the woman.

The village was four miles away, and once, and once again, the two on the ledge speculated as to the length of time it would take their companions to get back to the village; what men they were likely to find in the village at that time of day; how long it would take to explain what had happened, and finally, how long it would take the rescue party to arrive.

Conversation had been carried on in whispers for fear the tiger might be lurking in the vicinity and hear them, and then, suddenly, the woman gave a gasp and the girl, seeing the look of horror on her face and the direction in which she was looking, turned her head and over her shoulder saw the tiger, stepping out of the rift in the cliff on to the ledge.

Few of us, I imagine, have escaped that worst of all nightmares in which, while our limbs and vocal cords are paralysed with fear, some terrible beast in monstrous form approaches to destroy us; the nightmare from which, sweating fear in every pore, we waken with a cry of thankfulness to Heaven that it was only a dream. There was no such happy awakening from the nightmare of that unfortunate girl, and little imagination is needed to picture the scene. A rock cliff with a narrow ledge running partly across it and ending in a little depression in which an injured woman is lying; a young girl frozen wit h terror squatting on the ledge, and a tiger slowly creeping towards her; retreat in every direction cut off, and no help at hand.

Mothi Singh, an old friend of mine, was in the village visiting a sick daughter when the women arrived, and he headed the rescue party. When this party wen t down the grassy slope and looked over the diff, they saw the woman lying in a swoon, and on the ledge they saw splashes of blood.

The injured woman was carried back to the village, and when she had been revived and had told her story, Mothi Singh set out on his eighteen-mile walk to me. He was an old man well over sixty, but he scouted the suggestion that he was tired and needed a rest, so we set off together to make investigations. But there was nothing that I could do, for twenty-four hours had elapsed, and all that the tiger had left of the brave young girl who had volunteered to stay with her injured companion were a few bits of bone and her torn and bloodstained clothes.

This was the first human being killed by the tiger which later received recognition in Government records as 'The Mohan Man-Eater'.

After killing the girl, the tiger went down the Kosi valley for the winter, killing on its way – among other people – two men of the Public Works Department, and the daughter-in-law of our Member of the Legislative Council. As summer approached it returned to the scene of its first kill, and for several years thereafter its beat extended up and down the Kosi valley from Kakrighat to Gargia – a distance of roughly forty miles – until it finally took up its quarters on the hill above Mohan, in the vicinity of a village called Kartkanoula.

At the District Conference, to which reference has been made in a previous story, the three man-eating tigers operating at that time in the Kumaon Division were classed as follows in their order of importance:

> *1st: Chowgarh, Naini Tal District.*
> *2nd: Mohan, Almora District.*
> *3rd: Kanda, Garhwal District.*

After the Chowgarh tiger had been accounted for, I was reminded by Baines, Deputy Commissioner, Almora, that only a part of my promise made at the conference had been fulfilled, and that the Mohan tiger was next on the list. The tiger, he stated, was becoming more active and a greater menace every day, and had during the previous week killed three human beings, residents of Kartkanoula village. It was to this village Baines now suggested I should go.

While I had been engaged with the Chowgarh tiger, Baines had persuaded some sportsmen to go to Kartkanoula, but though they had sat up over human and animal kills they had failed to make contact with the man-eater and had returned to their depot at Ranikhet. Baines informed me I should now have the ground to myself – a very necessary precaution, for nerves wear thin when hunting man-caters, and accidents arc apt to result when two or more parties are hunting the same animal.

II

It was on a blistering hot day in May that I, my two servants, and the six Garhwalis I had brought with me from

Jim Corbett

Naini Tal alighted from the 1 p.m. train at Ramnagar and set off on our twenty-five-mile foot journey to Kartkanoula. Our first stage was only seven miles, but it was evening before we arrived at Gargia. I had left home in a hurry on receiving Baines' letter, and had not had time to ask for permission to occupy the Gargia Forest Bungalow, so I slept out in the open.

On the far side of the Kasi River at Gargia there is a cliff several hundred feet high, and while I was trying to get to sleep I heard what I thought were stones falling off the cliff on the rocks below. The sound was exactly the same as would be made by bringing two stones violently together. After some time this sound worried me, as sounds will on a hot night, and as the moon was up and the light good enough to avoid stepping on snakes, I left my camp-bed and set out to make investigations. I found that the sound was being made by a colony of frogs in a marsh by the side of the road. I have heard land-, water-, and tree-frogs making strange sounds in different parts of the world, but I have never heard anything so strange as the sound made by the frogs at Gargia in the month of May.

After a very early start next morning we did the twelve miles to Mohan before the sun got hot, and while my men were cooking their food and my servants were preparing my breakfast, the chokidar of the bungalow, two Forest Guards, and several men from the Mohan bazaar entertained me with stories of the man-eater, the most recent of which concerned the exploits of a fisherman who had been fishing the Kosi River. One of the Forest Guards claimed to be the proud hero of this exploit, and he described very graphically how he had been out one day with the fisherman and, on turning a bend in the river, they had come face to face with the man-eater; and how the fisherman had thrown away his rod and had grabbed the rifle off his – the Forest Guard's – shoulder; and how they had run for their lives with the tiger close on their heels. 'Did you look back?' I asked. 'No, sahib,' said he, pitying my ignorance. 'How could a man who was running for his life from a man-eater look back?'; and how the fisherman, who was leading by a head, in a thick patch of grass had fallen over a sleeping bear, after which there had been great confusion and shouting, and everyone, including the bear, had run in different directions and the fisherman had got lost; and how after a long time the fisherman had eventually found his way back to the bungalow and had said a lot to him – the Forest Guard – on the subject of having run away with his rifle and left him empty-handed to deal with a man-eating tiger and an angry bear. The Forest Guard ended up his recital by saying that the fisherman had left Mohan the following day, saying that he had hurt his leg when he fell over the bear, and that anyway there were no fish to be caught in the Kosi River.

By midday we were ready to continue our journey, and, with many warnings from the small crowd that had collected to see us off to keep a sharp look-out for the man-eater while going through the dense forest that lay ahead of us, we set out on our four-thousand-foot climb to Kartkanoula.

Our progress was slow, for my men were carrying heavy loads and the track was excessively steep, and the heat terrific. There had been some trouble in the upper villages a short time previously, necessitating the dispatch from Naini Tal of a small police force, and I had been advised to take everything I needed for myself and my men with me, as owing to the unsettled conditions it would not be possible to get any stores locally. This was the reason for the heavy loads my men were carrying.

After many halts we reached the edge of the cultivated land in the late afternoon, and as there was now no further danger to be apprehended for my men from the man-eater, I left them and set out alone for the Foresters' Hut, which is visible from Mohan, and which had been pointed out to me by the Forest Guards as the best place for my stay while at Kartkanoula.

The hut is on the ridge of the high hill overlooking Mohan, and as I approached it along the level stretch of road running across the face of the hill, in turning a corner in a ravine where there is some dense undergrowth, I came on a woman filling an earthenware pitcher from a little trickle of water flowing down a wooden trough. Apprehending that my approach on rubber-soled shoes would frighten her, I coughed to attract her attention, noticed that she started violently as I did so, and, a few yards beyond her, stopped to light a cigarette. A minute or two later I asked, without turning my head, if it was safe for anyone to be in this lonely spot, and after a little hesitation the woman answered that it was not safe, but that water had to be fetched and as there was no one in the home to accompany her, she had come alone. Was there no man? Yes, there was a man, but he was in the fields ploughing, and in any case it was the duty of women to fetch water. How long would it take to fill the pitcher? Only a little longer. The woman had got over her fright and shyness, and I was now subjected to a close cross-examination. Was I a policeman? No. Was I a Forest Officer? No. Then who was I? Just a man. Why had I come? To try and help the people of Kartkanoula. In what way? By shooting the man-eater. Where had I heard about the man-eater? – Why had I come alone? – Where were my men? – How many were there? – How long would I stay? And so on.

The pitcher was not declared full until the woman had satisfied her curiosity, and as she walked behind me she pointed to one of several ridges running down the south face of the hill, and pointing out a big tree growing on a grassy slope said that three days previously the man-eater had killed a woman under it; this tree, I noted with interest, was only two or three hundred yards from my objective – the Foresters' Hut. We had now come to a footpath running up the hill, and as she took it the woman said the village from which she had come was just round the shoulder of the hill, and added that she was now quite safe.

Those of you who know the women of India will realize that I had accomplished a lot, especially when it is remembered that there had recently been trouble in this area with the police. So far from alarming the woman and thereby earning the hostility of the entire countryside, I had, by standing by while she filled her pitcher and answering a few questions, gained a friend who would in the shortest time possible acquaint the whole population of the village of my arrival; that I was not an officer of any kind, and that the sole purpose of my visit was to try to rid them of the man-eater.

III

The Foresters' Hut was on a little knoll some twenty yards to the left of the road, and as the door was fastened only with a chain I opened it and walked inside. The room was about ten feet square and quite clean, but had a mouldy dis-used smell; I learnt that the hut had not been occupied since the advent of the man-eater in that area eighteen months previously. On either side of the main room there were two narrow slips of rooms, one used as a kitchen, and the other as a fuel store. The hut would make a nice safe shelter for my men, and having opened the back door to let a current of air blow through the room, I went outside and selected a spot between the hut and the road for my 40-lb. tent. There was no furniture of any kind in the hut, so I sat down on a rock near the road to await the arrival of my men.

The ridge at this point was about fifty yards wide, and as the hut was on the south edge of the ridge, and the village on the north face of the hill, the latter was not visible from the former. I had been sitting on the rock for about ten minutes when a head appeared over the crest from the direction of the village, followed by a second and a third. My friend the water-carrier had not been slow in informing the village of my arrival.

When strangers meet in India and wish to glean information from each other on any particular subject, it is customary to refrain from broaching the subject that has brought them together – whether accidentally or of set purpose – until the very last moment, and to fill up the interval by finding out everything concerning each other's domestic and private affairs; as, for instance, whether married and if so the number and sex of children and their ages; if not married, why not; occupation and amount of pay, and so on. Questions that would in any other part of the world earn one a thick ear are in India – and especially in our hills – asked so artlessly and universally that no one who has lived among the people dreams of taking offence at them.

In my conversation with the woman I had answered many of the set questions, and the ones of a domestic nature which it is not permissible for a woman to ask of a man were being put to me when my men arrived. They had filled a kettle at the little spring, and in an incredibly short time dry sticks were collected, a fire lit, the kettle boiled, and tea and biscuits produced. As I opened a tin of condensed milk I heard the men asking my servants why condensed milk was being used instead of fresh milk and receiving the answer that there was no fresh milk; and further that, as it had been apprehended that owing to some previous trouble in this area no fresh milk would be available, a large supply of tinned milk had been brought. The men appeared to be very distressed on hearing this, and after a whispered conversation one of them, who I learnt later was the Headman of Kartkanoula, addressed me and said it was an insult to them to have brought tinned milk, when all the resources of the village were at my disposal. I admitted my mistake, which I said was due to my being a stranger to that locality, and told the Headman that if he had any milk to spare I would gladly purchase a small quantity for my daily requirements, but that beyond the milk, I wanted for nothing.

My loads had now been unstrapped, while more men had arrived from the village, and when I told my servants where I wanted them to pitch my tent there was a horrified exclamation from the assembled villagers. Live in a tent – indeed! Was I ignorant of the fact that there was a man-eating tiger in this area and that it used this road regularly every night? If I doubted their word, let me come and see the claw marks on the doors of the houses where the road ran through the upper end of the village. Moreover, if the tiger did not eat me in the tent it would certainly eat my men in the hut, if I was not there to protect them. This last statement made my men prick up their ears and add their entreaties to the advice of the villagers, so eventually I agreed to stay in the main room, while my two servants occupied the kitchen, and the six Garhwalis the fuel store.

The subject of the man-eater having been introduced, it was now possible for me to pursue it without admitting that it was the one subject I had wished to introduce from the moment the first man had put his head over the ridge. The path leading down to the tree where the tiger had claimed its last victim was pointed out to me, and the time of day, and the circumstances under which the woman had been killed, explained. The road along which the tiger came every night, I was informed, ran eastward to Baital Ghat with a branch down to Mohan, and westward to Chaknakl on the Ramganga River. The road going west, after running through the upper part of the village and through cultivated land for half a mile, turned south along the face of the hill, and on rejoining the ridge on which the hut was, followed the ridge right down to Chaknakl. This portion of the road between Kartkanoula and Chaknakl, some six miles long, was considered to be very dangerous, and had not been used since the advent of the man-eater; I subsequently found that after leaving the cultivated land the road entered dense tree and scrub jungle, which extended right down to the river.

The main cultivation of Kartkanoula village is on the north face of the hill, and beyond this cultivated land there are several small ridges with deep ravines between. On the nearest of these ridges, and distant about a thousand yards from the Foresters' Hut, there is a big pine-tree. Near this tree, some ten days previously, the tiger had killed, partly eaten, and left a woman, and as the three sportsmen who were staying in a Forest Bungalow four miles away were unable to climb the pine-tree, the villagers had put up three machans in three separate trees, at distances varying from one hundred to one hundred and fifty yards from the kill, and the machans had been occupied by the sportsmen and their servants a little before sunset. There was a young moon at the time, and after it had set the villagers heard a number of shots being fired, and when they questioned the servants next morning the servants said they did not know what had been fired at, for they themselves had not seen anything. Two days later a cow had been killed over which the sportsmen had sat, and again, as on the previous occasion, shots had been fired after the moon had set. It is these admittedly sporting but unsuccessful attempts to bag man-eaters that makes them so wary, and the more difficult to shoot the longer they live.

The villagers gave me one very interesting item of news in connexion with the tiger. They said they always knew when it had come into the village by the low moaning sound it made. On questioning them closely I learnt that at times the sound was continuous as the tiger passed between the houses, while at other times the sound stopped for sometimes short and other times long periods.

From this information I concluded (a) that the tiger was suffering from a wound, (b) that the wound was of such a nature that the tiger only felt it when in motion, and that therefore (c) the wound was in one of its legs. I was assured that the tiger had not been wounded by any local shikari, or by any of the sportsmen from Ranikhet who had sat up for it; however, this was of little importance, for the tiger had been a man-eater for years, and the wound that I believed it was suffering from might have been the original cause of its becoming a man-eater. A very interesting point and one that could only be cleared up by examining the tiger – after it was dead.

The men were curious to know why I was so interested in the sound made by the tiger, and when I told them that it indicated the animal had a wound in one of its legs and that the wound had been caused either by a bullet or by porcupine quills, they disagreed with my reasoning and said that on the occasions they had seen the tiger it appeared to be in sound condition, and further, that the ease with which it killed and carried off its victims was proof that it was not crippled in any way. However, what I told them was remembered, and later earned me the reputation of being gifted with second sight.

IV

When passing through Ramnagar I had asked the Tashildar to purchase two young male buffaloes for me and to send them to Mohan, where my men would take them over.

I told the villagers I intended tying up one of the buffaloes near the tree where three days previously the woman had been killed and the other on the road to Chaknakl, and they said they could think of no better sites, but that they would talk the matter over among themselves and let me know in the morning if they had any other suggestions to make. Night was now drawing in, and before leaving the Headman promised to send word to all the adjoining villages in the morning to let them know of my arrival, the reason for my coming, and to impress on them the urgency of letting me know without loss of time of any kills or attacks by the tiger in their areas.

The musty smell in the room had much decreased, though it was still noticeable. However, I paid no attention to it, and after a bath and dinner put two stones against the doors – there being no other way of keeping them shut – and being bone-tired after my day's exertions went to bed and to sleep. I am a light sleeper, and two or three hours later I awoke on hearing an animal moving about in the jungle. It came right up to the back door. Getting hold of a rifle and a torch, I moved the stone aside with my foot and heard an animal moving off as I opened the door – it might from the sound it was making have been the tiger, but it might also have been a leopard or a porcupine. However, the jungle was too thick for me to see what it was. Back in the room and with the stone once more in position, I noticed I had developed a sore throat, which I attributed to having sat in the wind after the hot walk up from Mohan; but when my servant pushed the door open and brought in my early-morning cup of tea, I found I was suffering from an attack of laryngitis, due possibly to my having slept in a long-disused hut, the roof of which was swarming with bats. My servant informed me that he and his companion had escaped infection, but that the six Garhwalis in the fuel store were all suffering from the same complaint as I was. My stock of medicine consisted of a two-ounce bottle of iodine and a few tabloids of quinine, and on rummaging in my gun-case I found a small paper packet of permanganate, which my sister had provided for me on a previous occasion. The packet was soaked through with gun oil, but the crystals were still soluble, and I put a liberal quantity of the crystals into a tin of hot water, together with some iodine. The resulting gargle was very potent, and while it blackened our teeth it did much to relieve the soreness in our throats.

After an early breakfast I sent four men down to Mohan to bring up the two buffaloes, and myself set off to prospect the ground where the woman had been killed. From the directions I had received overnight I had no difficulty in finding the spot where the tiger had attacked and killed the woman as she was tying the grass she had cut into a bundle. The grass and the rope she was using were lying just as they had been left, as were also two bundles of grass left by her compa11io11s when they had run off in fright to the village. The men had told me that the body of the woman had not been found, but from the fact that three perfectly good lengths of rope and the dead woman's sickle had been left in the jungle, I am inclined to think that no attempt had been made to find her.

The woman had been killed at the upper end of a small landslide, and the tiger had taken her down the slide and into a thick patch of undergrowth. Here the tiger had waited, possibly to give the two women time to get out of sight, and had then crossed the ridge visible from the hut, after which it had gone with its kill straight down the hill for a mile or more into dense tree and scrub jungle. The tracks were now four days old, and as there was nothing to be gained by following them farther, I turned back to the hut.

The climb back to the ridge was a very steep one, and when I reached the hut at about midday I found an array of pots and pans of various shapes and sizes on the veranda, all containing milk. In contrast to the famine of the day before there was now abundance, sufficient milk in fact for me to have bathed in. My servants informed me they had protested to no effect and that each man had said, as he deposited his vessel on the veranda, that he would take good care that I used no more condensed milk while I remained in their midst.

I did not expect the men to return from Mohan with the buffaloes before nightfall, so after lunch I set out to have a look at the road to Chaknakl.

From the hut the hill sloped gradually upwards to a height of about five hundred feet, and was roughly triangular in shape. The road, after running through cultivated land for half a mile, turned sharply to the left, went across a steep rocky hill until it regained the ridge, and then turned to the right and followed the ridge down to Chaknakl. The road was level for a short distance after coming out on the ridge, and then went steeply down, the gradient in places being eased by hairpin bends.

I had the whole afternoon before me, and examined about three mites of the road very carefully. When a tiger uses a road regularly it invariably leaves signs of its passage by making scratch marks on the side of the road. These scratch marks, made for the same purpose as similar marks made by domestic cats and all other members of the cat family, are of very great interest to sportsmen, for they provide him with the following very useful information: (1) whether the animal that had made the marks is a male or a female, (2) the direction in which it was travelling, (3) the length of time that has elapsed since it passed, (4) the direction and approximate distance of its headquarters, (5) the nature of its kills, and finally, (6) whether the animal has recently had a meal of human flesh. The value of this easily acquired information to one who is hunting a man-eater on strange ground will be easily understood. Tigers also leave their pug-marks on the roads they use, and these pug-marks can provide one with quite a lot of useful information, as for instance the direction and speed at which the animal was travelling, its sex and age, whether all four limbs are sound, and, if not sound, which particular limb is defective.

The road I was on had through long disuse got overgrown with short stiff grass and was therefore not, except in one or two damp places, a good medium on which to leave pug-marks. One of these damp places was within a few yards of where the road came out on the ridge, and just below this spot there was a green and very stagnant pool of water; a regular drinking-place for sambur.

I found several scratch marks just round the corner where the road turned to the left after leaving the cultivated ground, the most recent of which was three days old. Two hundred yards from these scratch marks the road, for a third of its width, ran under an overhanging rock. This rock was ten feet high, and at the top there was a flat piece of ground two or three yards wide, which was only visible from the road when approaching the rock from the village side. On the ridge I found more scratch marks, but I did not find any pug-marks until I got to the first hairpin bend. Here, in cutting across the bend, the tiger had left its tracks where it had jumped down on to some soft earth. The tracks, which were a day old, were a little distorted, but even so it was possible to see that they had been made by a big, old, male tiger.

When one is moving in an area in which a man-eating tiger is operating, progress is of necessity very slow, for every obstruction in one's line of walk, be it a bush, a tree, a rock, or an inequality in the ground capable of concealing death, has to be cautiously approached, while at the same time, if a wind is not blowing – and there was no wind that evening – a careful and constant look-out has to be maintained behind and on either side. Further, there was much of interest to be looked at, for it was the month of May, when orchids at this elevation – 4,000 to 5,000 feet – are at their best, and I have never seen a greater variety or a greater wealth of bloom than the forests on that hill had to show. The beautiful white butterfly orchid was in greatest profusion, and every second tree of any size appeared to have decked itself out with them.

It was here that I first saw a bird that Prater, of the Bombay Natural History Society, later very kindly identified for me as the Mountain Crag Martin, a bird of a uniform ash colour, with a slight tinge of pink on its breast, and in size a little smaller than a Rosy Pastor. These birds had their broods with them, and while the young ones – four to a brood – sat in a row on a dry twig at the top of a high tree, the parent birds kept darting away – often to a distance of two or three hundred yards – to catch insects. The speed at which they flew was amazing, and I am quite sure there is nothing in feathers in North India, not excluding our winter visitor the great Tibetan Swallow, that these Martins could not make rings round. Another thing about these birds that was very interesting was their wonderful eyesight. On occasions they would fly in a dead straight line for several hundred yards before turning and coming back. It was not possible, at the speed they were going, that they were chasing insects on flights, and as after each flight the bird invariably thrust some minute object into one of the gaping mouths, I believe they were able to see insects at a range at which they would not have been visible to the human eye through the most powerful field-glasses.

Safeguarding my neck, looking out for tracks, enjoying nature generally, and listening to all the jungle sounds – a sambur a mile away down the hill-side in the direction of Mohan was warning the jungle folk of the presence of a tiger, and a kakar and a langur (Entellus monkey) on the road to Chaknakl were warning other jungle folk of the presence of a leopard – time passed quickly, and I found myself back at the overhanging rock as the sun was setting. As I approached this rock I marked it as being quite the most dangerous spot in all the ground I had so far gone over. A tiger lying on the grass-covered bit of ground above the rock would only have to wait until anyone going either up or down the road was under or had passed it to have them at his mercy – a very dangerous spot indeed and one that needed remembering.

When I got back to the hut I found the two buffaloes had arrived, but it was too late to do anything with them that evening.

My servants had kept a fire going most of the day in the hut, the air of which was now sweet and clean, but even so I was not going to risk sleeping in a closed room again; so I made them cut two thorn bushes and wedged them firmly into the doorways before going to bed. There was no movement in the jungle near the back door that night, and after a sound sleep I woke in the morning with my throat very much better.

I spent most of the morning talking to the village people and listening to the tales they had to tell of the man-eater and the attempts that had been made to shoot it, and after lunch I tied up one buffalo on the small ridge the tiger had crossed when carrying away the woman, and the other at the hairpin bend where I had seen the pug-marks.

Next morning I found both buffaloes sleeping peacefully after having eaten most of the big feed of grass I had provided them with. I had tied bells round the necks of both animals, and the absence of any sound from these bells as I approached each buffalo gave me two disappointments, for, as I have said, I found both of them asleep. That evening I changed the position of the second buffalo from the hairpin bend to where the road came out on the ridge, close to the pool of stagnant water.

The methods most generally employed in tiger shooting can briefly be described as (a) sitting up, and (b) beating, and young male buffaloes are used as bait in both cases. The procedure followed is to select the area most convenient for a sit-up, or for a beat, and to tie the bait out in the late evening, using a rope which the bait cannot, but which the tiger can, break; and when the bait is taken, either to sit up over the kill on a machan in a tree or beat the cover into which the kill has been taken.

In the present case neither of these methods was feasible. My throat, though very much better, was still sore, and it would not have been possible for me to have sat up for any length of time without coughing, and a beat over that vast area of heavily wooded and broken ground would have been hopeless even if I had been able to muster a thousand men; so I decided to stalk the tiger, and to this end carefully sited my two buffaloes and tied them to stout saplings with four one-inch-thick hemp ropes, and left them out in the jungle for the whole twenty-four hours.

I now stalked the buffaloes in turn each morning, as soon as there was sufficient light to shoot by, and again in the evening; for tigers, be they man-eaters or not, kill as readily in the day as they do at night in areas in which they are not disturbed; and during the day, while I waited for news from outlying villages, nursed my throat, and rested, my six Garhwalis fed and watered the buffaloes.

On the fourth evening when I was returning at sunset after visiting the buffalo on the ridge, as I came round a bend in the road thirty yards from the overhanging rock, I suddenly, and for the first time since my arrival at Kartkanoula, felt I was in danger, and that the danger that threatened me was on the rock in front of me. For five minutes I stood perfectly still with my eyes fixed on the upper edge of the rock, watching for movement. At that short range the flicker of an eyelid would have caught my eyes, but there was not even this small movement; and after going forward ten paces, I again stood watching for several minutes. The fact that I had seen no movement did not in any way reassure me – the man-eater was on the rock, of that I was sure; and the question was, what was I going to do about it? The hill, as I have already told you, was very steep, had great rocks jutting out of it, and was overgrown with long grass and tree and scrub jungle. Bad as the going was, had it been earlier in the day I would have gone back and worked round and above the tiger to try to get a shot at him; but with only half an hour of daylight left, and the best part of a mile still to go, it would have been madness to have left the road. So, slipping up the safety-catch and putting the rifle to my shoulder, I started to pass the rock.

The road here was about eight feet wide, and going to the extreme outer edge I started walking crab-fashion, feeling each step with my feet before putting my weight down to keep from stepping off into space. Progress was slow and difficult, but as I drew level with the overhanging rock and then began to pass it, hope rose high that the tiger would remain where he was until I reached that part of the road from which the flat bit of ground above the rock, on which he was lying, was visible. The tiger, however, having failed to catch me off my guard, was taking no chances, and I had just got clear of the rock when I heard a low muttered growl above me, and a little later first a kakar went off barking to the right, and then two hind sambur started belling near the crest of the triangular hill.

The tiger had got away with a sound skin, but, for the matter of that, so had I, so there was no occasion for regrets, and from the place on the hill where the sambur said he was, I felt sure he would hear the bell I had hung round the neck of the buffalo that was tied on the ridge near the stagnant pool.

When I reached the cultivated land I found a group of men waiting for me. They had heard the kakar and sambur and were very disappointed that I had not seen the tiger, but cheered up when I told them I had great hopes for the morrow.

V

During the night a dust-storm came on, followed by heavy rain, and I found to my discomfort that the roof of the hut was very porous. However, I eventually found a spot where it was leaking less than in others, dragged my camp-bed to it, and continued my sleep. It was a brilliantly clear morning when I awoke; the rain had washed the heat haze and dust out of the atmosphere, and every leaf and blade of grass was glistening in the newly risen sun.

Hitherto I had visited the nearer buffalo first, but this morning I had an urge to reverse the daily procedure, and after instructing my men to wait until the sun was well up and then go to feed and water the nearer buffalo, I set off with high hopes down the Chaknakl road, having first cleaned and oiled my 450/400 rifle – a very efficient weapon, and a good and faithful friend of many years' standing.

The overhanging rock that I had passed with such trouble the previous evening did not give me a moment's uneasiness now, and after passing it I started looking for tracks, for the rain had softened the surface of the road. I saw nothing, however, until I came to the damp place on the road, which, as I have said, was on the near side of the ridge and close to the pool where the buffalo was tied. Here in the soft earth I found the pug-marks of the tiger, made before the storm had come on, and going in the direction of the ridge. Close to this spot there is a rock about three feet high, on the khud side of the road. On the previous occasions that I had stalked down the road I had found that by standing on this rock I could look over a hump in the road and see the buffalo where it was tied forty yards away. When I now climbed on to the rock and slowly raised my head, I found that the buffalo had gone. This discovery was as disconcerting as it was inexplicable. To prevent the tiger from carrying the buffalo away to some distant part of the jungle, where the only method of getting a shot would have been by sitting up on the ground or in a tree – a hopeless proceeding with my throat in the condition it was in – I had used four thicknesses of strong one-inch-thick hemp rope, and even so the tiger had got away with the kill.

I was wearing the thinnest of rubber-soled shoes, and very silently I approached the sapling to which the buffalo had been tied and examined the ground. The buffalo had been killed before the storm, but had been carried away after the rain had stopped, without any portion of it having been eaten. Three of the ropes I had twisted together had been gnawed through, and the fourth had been broken. Tigers do not usually gnaw through ropes; however, this one had done so, and had carried off the kill down the hill facing Mohan. My plans had been badly upset, but very fortunately the rain had come to my assistance. The thick carpet of dead leaves which the day before had been as dry as tinder were now wet and pliable, and, provided I made no mistakes, the pains the tiger had been to in getting away with the kill might yet prove his undoing.

When entering a jungle in which rapid shooting might at any moment become necessary, I never feel happy until I have reassured myself that my rifle is loaded. To pull a trigger in an emergency and wake up in the Happy Hunting Grounds – or elsewhere – because one had omitted to load a weapon, would be one of those acts of carelessness for which no excuse could be found; so though I knew I had loaded my rifle before I came to the overhanging rock, I now opened it and extracted the cartridges. I changed one that was discoloured and dented, and after moving the safety-catch up and down several times to make sure it was working smoothly – I have never carried a cocked weapon – I set off to follow the drag.

This word 'drag', when it is used to describe the mark left on the ground by a tiger when it is moving its kill from one place to another, is misleading, for a tiger when taking its kill any distance (I have seen a tiger carry a full-grown cow for four miles) does not drag it, it carries it; and if the kill is too heavy to be carried, it is left. The drag is distinct or faint according to the size of the animal that is being carried, and the manner in which it is being held. For instance, assuming the kill is a sambur and the tiger is holding it by the neck, the hind quarters will trail on the ground leaving a distinct drag mark. On the other hand, if the sambur is being held by the middle of the back, there may be a faint drag mark, or there may be none at all.

In the present case the tiger was carrying the buffalo by the neck, and the hind quarters trailing on the ground were leaving a drag mark it was easy to follow. For a hundred yards the tiger went diagonally across the face of the hill until he came to a steep clay bank. In attempting to cross this bank he had slipped and relinquished his hold of the kill, which had rolled down the hill for thirty or forty yards until it had fetched up against a tree. On recovering the kill the tiger picked it up by the back, and from now on only one leg occasionally touched the ground, leaving a faint drag mark, which nevertheless, owing to the hill-side's being carpeted with bracken, was not very difficult to follow. In his fall the tiger had lost direction, and now appeared to be undecided where to take the kill. First he went a couple of hundred yards to the right, then a hundred yards straight down the hill through a dense patch of ringals (stunted bamboo). After forcing his way with considerable difficulty through the ringals, he turned to the left and went diagonally across the hill for a few hundred yards until he came to a great rock, to the right of which he skirted. This rock was flush with the ground on the approach side, and, rising gently for twenty feet, appeared to project out over a hollow or dell of considerable extent. If there was a cave or recess under the projection, it would be a very likely place for the tiger to have taken his kill to, so leaving the drag I stepped on to the rock and moved forward very slowly, examining every yard of ground below and on either side of me, as it came into view. On reaching the end of the projection and looking over I was disappointed to find that the hill came up steeply to meet the rock, and that there was no cave or recess under it as I had expected there would be.

As the point of the rock offered a good view of the dell and of the surrounding jungle – and was comparatively safe from an attack from the man-eater – I sat down; and as I did so, I caught sight of a red-and-white object in a dense patch of short undergrowth, forty or fifty yards directly below me. When one is looking for a tiger in heavy jungle everything red that catches the eye is immediately taken for the tiger, and here, not only could I see the red of the tiger, but I could also see his stripes. For a long minute I watched the object intently, and then, as the face you are told to look for in a freak picture suddenly resolves itself, I saw that the object I was looking at was the kill, and not the tiger; the red was blood where he had recently been eating, and the stripes were the ribs from which he had torn away the skin. I was thankful for having held my fire for that long minute, for in a somewhat similar case a friend of mine ruined his chance of bagging a very fine tiger by putting two bullets into a kill over which he had intended sitting; fortunately he was a good shot, and the two men whom he had sent out in advance to find the kill and put up a machan over it, and who were, at the time he fired, standing near the kill screened by a bush, escaped injury.

When a tiger that has not been disturbed leaves his kill out in the open, it can be assumed that he is lying up close at hand to guard that kill from vultures and other scavengers, and the fact that I could not see the tiger did not mean that he was not lying somewhere close by in the dense undergrowth.

Tigers arc troubled by flies and do not lie long in one position, so I decided to remain where I was and watch for movement; but hardly had I come to this decision, when I felt an irritation in my throat. I had not quite recovered from my attack of laryngitis, and the irritation grew rapidly worse until it became imperative for me to cough. The usual methods one employs on these occasions, whether in church or the jungle, such as holding the breath and swallowing hard, gave no relief until it became a case of cough, or burst; and in desperation I tried to relieve my throat by giving the alarm-call of the langur. Sounds are difficult to translate into words, and for those of you who are not acquainted with our jungles I would try to describe this alarm-call, which can be heard for half a mile, *as khok, khok, khok* , repeated again and again at short intervals, and ending up with *khokorror*. All langurs do not call at tigers, but the ones in our hills certainly do, and as this tiger had probably heard the call every day of his life it was the one sound I could make to which he would not pay the slightest attention. My rendering of the call in this emergency did not sound very convincing, but it had the desired effect of removing the irritation from my throat.

For half an hour thereafter I continued to sit on the rock, watching for movement and listening for news from the jungle folk, and when I had satisfied myself that the tiger was not anywhere within my range of vision, I got off the rock, and, moving with the utmost caution, went down to the kill.

VI

I regret I am not able to tell you what weight of flesh a full-grown tiger can consume at a meal, but you will have some idea of his capacity when I tell you he can eat a sambur in two days, and a buffalo in three, leaving possibly a small snack for the fourth day.

The buffalo I had tied up was not full-grown, but he was by no means a small animal, and the tiger had eaten approximately half of him. With a meal of that dimension inside of him I felt sure he had not gone far, and as the ground was still wet, and would remain so for another hour or two, I decided to find out in what direction he had gone, and if possible, stalk him.

There were a confusion of tracks near the kill, but by going round in widening circles I found the track the tiger had made when leaving. Soft-footed animals are a little more difficult to track than hard-footed ones, yet after long years of experience tracking needs as little effort as a gun-dog exerts when following a scent. As silently and as slowly as a shadow, I took up the track, knowing that the tiger would be close at hand. When I had gone a hundred yards I came on a flat bit of ground, twenty feet square, and carpeted with that variety of short soft grass that has highly scented roots; on this grass the tiger had lain, the imprint of his body being clearly visible.

As I was looking at the imprint and guessing at the size of the animal that had made it, I saw some of the blades of grass that had been crushed down spring erect.   T h i s indicated that the tiger had been gone only a minute or so.

You will have some idea of the lay-out when I tell you that the tiger had brought the kill down from the north, and on leaving it had gone west, and that the rock on which I had sat, the kill, and the spot where I was now standing formed the points of a triangle, one side of which was forty yards, and the other two sides a hundred yards long.

My first thought on seeing the grass spring erect was that the tiger had seen me and moved off, but this I soon found was not likely, for neither the rock nor the kill was visible from the grass plot, and that he had not seen me and moved after I had taken up his track I was quite certain. Why then had he left his comfortable bed and gone away? The sun shining on the back of my neck provided the answer. It was now nine o'clock of an unpleasantly hot May morning, and a glance at the sun and the tree-tops over which it had come showed that it had been shining on the grass for ten minutes. The tiger had evidently found it too hot, and gone away a few minutes before my arrival to look for a shady spot.

I have told you that the grass plot was twenty feet square. On the far side to that from which I had approached there was a fallen tree, lying north and south. This tree was about four feet in diameter, and as it was lying along the edge of the grass plot in the middle of which I was standing, it was ten feet away from me. The root end of the tree was resting on the hill-side, which here went up steeply and was overgrown with brushwood, and the branch end (which had been snapped off when the tree had fallen) was projecting out over the hill-side. Beyond the tree the hill appeared to be more or less perpendicular, and running across the face of it was a narrow ledge of rock, which disappeared into dense jungle thirty yards farther on.

If my surmise, that the sun had been the cause of the tiger's changing his position, was correct, there was no more suitable place than the lee of the tree for him to have taken shelter in, and the only way of satisfying myself 011 this point was to walk up to the tree – and look over. Here a picture seen long years ago in Punch flashed into memory. The picture was of a lone sportsman who had gone out to hunt lions and who, on glancing up on to the rock he was passing, looked straight into the grinning face of the most enormous lion in Africa. Underneath the picture was written, 'When you go out looking for a lion, be quite sure that you want to see him'. True, there would be this small difference, that whereas my friend in Africa looked up – into the lion's face, I would look down – into the tiger's; otherwise the two cases – assuming that the tiger was on the far side of the tree – would be very similar.

Slipping my feet forward an inch at a time on the soft grass, I now started to approach the tree, and had covered about half the distance that separated me from it when I caught sight of a black-and-yellow object about three inches long on the rocky ledge, which I now saw was a well-used game-path. For a long minute I stared at this motionless object, until I was convinced that it was the tip of the tiger's tail. If the tail was pointing away from me the head must obviously be towards me, and as the ledge was only some two feet wide, the tiger could only be crouching down and waiting to spring the moment my head appeared over the bole of the tree. The tip of the tail was twenty feet from me, and allowing eight feet for the tiger's length while crouching, his head would be twelve feet away. But I should have to approach much nearer before I should be able to see enough of his body to get in a crippling shot, and a crippling shot it would have to be if I wanted to leave on my feet. And now, for the first time in my life, I regretted my habit of carrying an uncocked rifle. The safety-catch of my 450/400 makes a very distinct click when thrown off, and to make any sound now would either bring the tiger right on top of me or send him straight down the steep hillside without any possibility of my getting in a shot.

Inch by inch I again started to creep forward, until the whole of the tail, and after it the hind quarters, came into view. When I saw the hind quarters I could have shouted with delight, for they showed that the tiger was not crouching and ready to spring, but was lying down. As there was only room for his body on the two-foot-wide ledge, he had stretched his hind legs out and was resting them on the upper branches of an oak-sapling growing up the face of the almost perpendicular hill-side. Another foot forward and his belly came into view, and from the regular way in which it was heaving up and down I knew that he was asleep. Less slowly now I moved forward, until his shoulder, and then his whole length, was exposed to my view. The back of his head was resting on the edge of the grass plot, which extended for three or four feet beyond the fallen tree; his eyes were fast shut, and his nose was pointing to heaven.

Aligning the sights of the rifle on his forehead I pressed the trigger and, while maintaining a steady pressure on it, pushed up the safety-catch. I had no idea how this reversal of the usual method of discharging a rifle would work, but it did work; and when the heavy bullet at that short range crashed into his forehead not so much as a quiver went through his body. His tail remained stretched straight out; his hind legs continued to rest on the upper branches of the sapling; and his nose still pointed to heaven. Nor did his position change in the slightest when I sent a second, and quite unnecessary, bullet to follow the first. The only change noticeable was that his stomach had stopped heaving up and down, and that blood was trickling down his forehead from two surprisingly small holes.

I do not know how the close proximity of a tiger reacts on others, but me it always leaves with a breathless feeling – due possibly as much to fear as to excitement – and a desire for a little rest. I sat down on the fallen tree and lit the cigarette I had denied myself from the day my throat had got bad, and allowed my thoughts to wander. Any task well accomplished gives satisfaction, and the one just completed was no exception. The reason for my presence at that spot was the destruction of the man-eater, and from the time I had left the road two hours previously right up to the moment I pushed up the safety-catch, everything – including the langur call – had worked smoothly and without a single fault. In this there was great satisfaction, the kind of satisfaction I imagine an author must feel when he writes *Finis* to the plot that, stage by stage, has unfolded itself just as he desired it to. In my case, however, the finish had not been satisfactory, for I had killed the animal, that was lying five feet from me, in his sleep.

My personal feelings in the matter are I know of little interest to others, but it occurs to me that possibly you also might think it was not cricket, and in that case I should like to put the arguments before you that I used on myself, in the hope that you will find them more satisfactory than I did. These arguments were (a) the tiger was a man-eater that was better dead than alive, (b) therefore it made no difference whether he was awake or asleep when killed, and (c) that had I walked away when I saw his belly heaving up and down I should have been morally responsible for the deaths of all the human beings he killed thereafter. All good and sound arguments, you will admit, for my having acted as I did; but the regret remains that through fear of the consequences to myself, or fear of losing the only chance I might ever get, or possibly a combination of the two, I did not awaken the sleeping animal and give him a sporting chance.

The tiger was dead, and if my trophy was to be saved

from falling into the valley below and ruined, it was advisable to get him off the ledge with as little delay as possible. Leaning the rifle, for which I had no further use, against the fallen tree, I climbed up to the road and, once round the corner near the cultivated land, I cupped my hands and sent a cooee echoing over the hills and valleys. I had no occasion lo repeat the call, for my men had heard my two shots when returning from attending to the first buffalo and had run back to the hut to collect as many villagers as were within calling distance. Now, on hearing my cooee, the whole crowd came helter-skelter down the road to meet me.

When stout ropes and an axe had been procured I took the crowd back with me, and after I had secured the ropes round the tiger, willing hands half-carried and half-dragged him off the ledge and over the fallen tree, on to the plot of grass. Here I would have skinned him, but the villagers begged me not to do so, saying that the women and children of Kartkanoula and the adjoining villages would be very disappointed if they were not given an opportunity of seeing the tiger with their own eyes and satisfying themselves that the man-eater, in fear of whom they had lived for so many years, and who had established a reign of terror over the whole district, was really and truly dead.

While a couple of saplings to assist in carrying the tiger back to the hut were being felled, I saw some of the men passing their hands over the tiger's limbs, and knew they were satisfying themselves that their assertion that the tiger had not been suffering from any old, or crippling, wounds was correct. At the hut the tiger was placed in the shade of a wide-spreading tree, and the villagers were informed that it was at their disposal up to two o'clock – longer I could not give them, for it was a very hot day and there was fear of the hair slipping, and the skin being ruined.

I myself had not looked closely at the tiger, but at 2 p.m., when I laid him on his back to start the skinning, I noticed that most of the hair from the inner side of his left foreleg was missing, and that there were a number of small punctures in the skin, from which yellow fluid was exuding. I did not draw attention to these puncture!!, and left the skinning of the leg, which was considerably thinner than the right leg, to the last. When the skin had been removed from the rest of the animal, I made a long cut from the chest to the pad of the festering left leg, and as I removed the skin, drew out of the flesh, one after another, porcupine quills which the men standing round eagerly seized as souvenirs; the longest of these quills was about five inches, and their total number was between twenty-five and thirty. The flesh under the skin, from the tiger's chest to the pad of his foot, was soapy, and of a dark yellow colour; cause enough to have made the poor beast moan when he walked, and quite sufficient reason for his having become – and having remained – a man-eater, for porcupine quills do not dissolve no matter how long they are embedded in flesh.

I have extracted, possibly, a couple of hundred porcupine quills from the man-eating tigers I have shot. Many of these quills have been over nine inches in length and as thick as pencils. The majority were embedded in hard muscles, a few were wedged firmly between bones, and all were broken off short under the skin.

Unquestionably the tigers acquired the quills when killing porcupines for food, but the question arises – to which I regret I am unable to give any satisfactory answer – why animals with the intelligence, and the agility, of tigers should be so careless as to drive quills deep into themselves, or be so slow in their movements as to permit porcupines – whose only method of defending themselves is by walking backwards – to do so; and further, why the quills should have been broken off short, for porcupine quills are not brittle.

Leopards are just as partial to porcupines as our hill tigers are, but they do not get quills stuck in them, for they kill porcupines – as I have seen – by catching them by the head; and why tigers do not employ the same safe and obvious method of killing as leopards employ, and so avoid injury to themselves, is a mystery to me.

And now I have done telling you the story of the second of the three man-eating tigers mentioned at that District Conference of long ago and, when opportunity offers, I will tell you how the third tiger, the Kanda man-eater, died.

THE FISH OF MY DREAMS

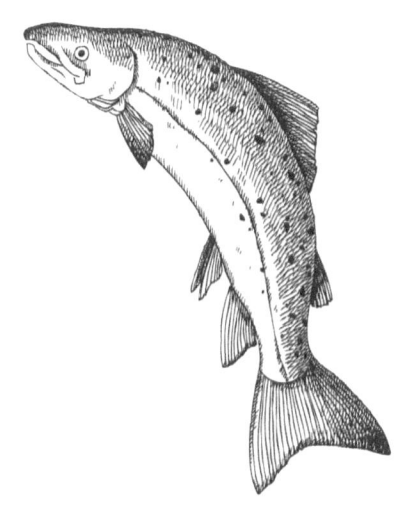

Fishing for mahseer in a well-stocked submontane river is, in my opinion, the most fascinating of all field sports. Our environments, even though we may not be continuously conscious of them, nevertheless play a very important part in the sum total of our enjoyment of any form of outdoor sport. I am convinced that the killing of the fish of one's dreams in uncongenial surroundings would afford an angler as little pleasure as the winning of the Davis Cup would to a tennis player if the contest were staged in the Sahara.

The river I have recently been fishing in flows, for some forty miles of its length, through a beautifully wooded valley, well stocked with game and teeming with bird life. I had the curiosity to count the various kinds of animals and birds seen in one day, and by the evening of that day my count showed, among animals, sambur, chital, kakar, ghooral, pig, langur, and red monkeys; and among birds, seventy-five varieties including pea-fowl, red jungle fowl, kaleege pheasants, black partridge, and bush quail.

In addition to these I saw a school of five otter in the river, several small mugger, and a python. The python was lying on the surface of a big still pool, with only the top of its flat head and eyes projecting above the gin-clear water. The subject was one I had long wished to photograph, and in order to do this it was necessary to cross the river above the pool and climb the opposite hill-side; but unfortunately

I had been seen by those projecting eyes, and as I cautiously stepped backwards, the reptile, which appeared to be about eighteen feet long, submerged, to retire to its subterranean home among the piled-up boulders at the head of the pool.

In some places the valley through which the river flows is so narrow that a stone can be tossed with ease from one side to the other, and in other places it widens out to a mile or more. In these open spaces grow amaltas with their two-feet-long sprays of golden bloom, karaunda, and box bushes with their white, star-shaped flowers. The combined scent from these flowers fills the air, throbbing with the spring songs of a multitude of birds, with the most delicate and pleasing of perfumes. In these surroundings angling for mahseer might well be described as sport fit for kings. My object in visiting this sportsman's paradise was not, however, to kill mahseer, but to try to secure a daylight picture of a tiger, and it was only when light conditions were unfavourable that I laid aside my movie camera for a rod.

I had been out from dawn one day, trying, hour after hour, to get a picture of a tigress and her two cubs. The tigress was a young animal, nervous as all young mothers are, and as often as I stalked her she retired with the cubs into heavy cover. There is a limit to the disturbance a tigress, be she young or old, will suffer when accompanied by cubs, and when the limit on this occasion had been reached I altered my tactics and tried sitting up in trees over open glades, and lying in high grass near a stagnant pool in which she and her family were accustomed to drink, but with no better success.

When the declining sun was beginning to cast shadows over the open places I was watching, I gave up the attempt, and added the day to the several hundred days I had already spent in trying to get a picture of a tiger in its natural surroundings. The two men I had brought from camp had passed the day in the shade of a tree on the far side of the river. I instructed them to return to camp by way of the forest track, and, exchanging my camera for a rod, set off alone along the river, intent on catching a fish for my dinner.

The fashion in rods and tackle has altered, in recent years, as much as the fashion in ladies' dress. Gone, one often wonders where, are the eighteen-foot greenheart rods with their unbreakable accompaniments, and gone the muscles to wield them, and their place has been taken by light, one-handed fly rods.

I was armed with an eleven-foot tournament trout rod, a reel containing fifty yards of casting line and 200 yards of fine silk backing, a medium gut cast, and a one-inch home-made brass spoon.

When one has unlimited, undisturbed water to fish, one is apt to be over-critical. A pool is discarded because the approach to it is over rough ground, or a run is rejected because of a suspected snag. On this occasion, half a mile had been traversed before a final selection was made; a welter of white water cascading over rocks at the head of a deep oily run eighty yards long, and at the end of the run a deep still pool two hundred yards long and seventy yards wide. Here was the place to catch the fish for my dinner.

Standing just clear of the white water, I flicked the spoon into the run, pulling a few yards of line off the reel as I did so, and as I raised the rod to allow the line to run through the rings the spoon was taken by a fish, near the bank, and close to where I was standing. By great good luck the remaining portion of the slack line tightened on the drum of the reel and did not foul the butt of the rod or handle of the reel, as so often happens.

In a flash the fish was off downstream, the good, well-oiled reel singing a paean of joy as the line was stripped off it. The fifty yards of casting line followed by a hundred yards of backing were gone, leaving in their passage burned furrows in the fingers of my left hand, when all at once the mad rush ceased as abruptly as it had begun, and the line went dead.

The speculations one makes on these occasions chased each other through my mind, accompanied by a little strong language to ease my feelings. The hold had been good without question. The cast, made up a few days previously from short lengths of gut procured from the Pilot Gut Company, had been carefully tied and tested. Suspicion centred on the split ring: possibly, cracked on a stone on some previous occasion, it had now given way.

Sixty yards of the line are back on the reel, when the slack line is seen to curve to the left, and a moment later is cutting a strong furrow upstream – the fish is still on, and is heading for the white water. Established here, pulling lternately from upstream, at right angles, and downstream fails to dislodge him. Time drags on, and the conviction grows that the fish has gone, leaving the line hung up on a snag. Once again and just as hope is being abandoned tl1e line goes slack, and then tightens a moment later, as the fish for the second time goes madly downstream.

And now he appears to have made up his mind to leave this reach of the river for the rapids below the pool. In one strong steady run he reaches the tail of the pool. Here, where the water fans out and shallows, he hesitates, and finally returns to the pool. A little later he shows on the surface for the first time, and but for the fact that the taut line runs direct from the point of the rod to the indistinctly seen object on the far side of the pool, it would be impossible to believe that the owner of that great triangular fin, projecting five inches out of the water, had taken a fly spoon a yard or two from my feet.

Back in the depths of the pool, he was drawn inch by inch into slack water. To land a big fish single-handed on a trout rod is not an easy accomplishment. Four times he was stranded with a portion of his great shoulders out of water, and four times at my very cautious approach he lashed out, and, returning to the pool, had to be fought back inch by inch. At the fifth attempt, with the butt of the rod held in the crook of my thumb and reversed, rings upwards to avoid the handle of the reel coming into contact with him, he permits me to place one hand and then the other against his sides and very gently propel him through the shallow water up on to dry land.

A fish I had set out to catch, and a fish I had caught, but he would take no part in my dinner that night, for between me and camp lay three and a half miles of rough ground, half of which would have to be covered in the dark.

When sending away my eleven-pound camera I had retained the cotton cord I use for drawing it up after me when I sit in trees. One end of this cord was passed through the gills of the fish and out at his mouth, and securely tied in a loop. The other end was made fast to the branch of a tree. When the cord was paid out, the fish lay snugly against a great slab of rock, in comparatively still water. Otter were the only danger, and to scare them off I made a flag of my handkerchief, and fixed the end of the improvised flagstaff in the bed of the river a little below the fish.

The sun was gilding the mountain-tops next morning when I was back at the pool, and found the fish lying just where I had left it the previous evening. Having unfastened the cord from the branch, I wound it round my hand as I descended the slab of rock towards the fish. Alarmed at my approach, or feeling the vibration of the cord, the fish suddenly galvanized into life, and with a mighty splash dashed upstream. Caught at a disadvantage, I had no time to brace my feet on the sloping and slippery rock, but was jerked headlong into the pool.

I have a great distaste for going over my depth in these submontane rivers, for the thought of being encircled by a hungry python is very repugnant to me, and I am glad there were no witnesses to the manner in which I floundered out of that pool. I had just scrambled out on the far side, with the fish still attached to my right hand, when the men I had instructed to follow me arrived. Handing the fish over to them to take down to our camp on the bank of the river, I went ahead to change and get my camera ready.

I had no means of weighing the fish and at a rough guess both the men and I put it at fifty pounds.

The weight of the fish is immaterial, for weights are soon forgotten. Not so forgotten are the surroundings in which the sport is indulged in. The steel blue of the fern-fringed pool where the water rests a little before cascading over rock and shingle to draw breath again in another pool more beautiful than the one just left – the flash of the gaily coloured kingfisher as he breaks the surface of the water, shedding a shower of diamonds from his wings as he rises with a chirp of delight, a silver minnow held firmly in his vermilion bill – the belling of the sambur and the clear tuneful call of the chital apprising the jungle folk that the tiger, whose pug-marks show wet on the sand where a few minutes before he crossed the river, is out in search of his dinner. These are things that will not be forgotten and will live in my memory, the lodestone to draw me back to that beautiful valley, as yet unspoiled by the hand of man.

THE KANDA
MAN-EATER

However little faith we have in the superstitions we share with others – thirteen at a table, the passing of wine at dinner, walking under a ladder, and so on – our own private superstitions, though a source of amusement to our friends, are very real to us.

I do not know if sportsmen arc more superstitious than the rest of mankind, but I do know that they take their superstitions very seriously. One of my friends invariably takes five cartridges, never more and never less, when he goes out after big game, and another as invariably takes seven cartridges. Another, who incidentally was the best-known big-game sportsman in Northern India, never started the winter shooting season without first killing a mahseer. My own private superstition concerns snakes. When after man-eaters I have a deep-rooted conviction that, however much I may try, all my efforts will be unavailing until I have first killed a snake.

During the hottest days of one May I had from dawn to dark climbed innumerable miles up and down incredibly steep hills, and through thick thorn bushes that had left my hands and knees a mass of ugly scratches, in search of a very wary man-eater. I returned on that fifteenth evening, dog-tired, to the two-room Forest Bungalow I was staying at, to find a deputation of villagers waiting for me with the very welcome news that the man-eater, a tiger, had been seen that day on the outskirts of their village. It was too late to do anything that night, so the deputation were provided with lanterns and sent home with strict injunctions that no one was to leave the village the following day.

The village was situated at the extreme end of the ridge on which the bungalow was, and because of its isolated position and the thick forest that surrounded it had suffered more from the depredations of the tiger than any other village in the district. The most recent victims were two women and a man.

I had made one complete circle of the village the following morning and had done the greater part of a second circle, a quarter of a mile below the first, when after negotiating a difficult scree of shale I came on a little nullah made by the rush of rain-water down the steep hill-side. A glance up and down the nullah satisfied me that the tiger was not in it, and then a movement just in front of me, and about twenty-five feet away, caught my eye. At this spot there was a small pool of water the size of a bathtub, and on the far side of it was a snake that had evidently been drinking. The lifting of the snake's head had caught my eye, and it was not until the head had been raised some two or three feet from the ground and the hood expanded that I realized it was a hamadryad. It was the most beautiful snake I had ever seen. The throat, as it faced me, was a deep orange red shading to golden-yellow where the body met the ground. The back, olive green, was banded by ivory-coloured chevrons, and some four feet of its length from the tip of its tail upwards was shiny black, with white chevrons. In length the snake was between thirteen and fourteen feet.

One hears many tales about hamadryads, their aggressiveness when disturbed, and the speed at which they can travel. If, as it seemed about to do, the snake attacked up or down hill I should be at a disadvantage, but across the shale scree I felt that I could hold my own. A shot at the expanded hood, the size of a small plate, would have ended the tension, but the rifle in my hands was a heavy one, and I had no intention of disturbing the tiger that had showed up after so many days of weary waiting and toil. After an interminably long minute, during which time the only movement was the flicking in and out of a Jong and quivering forked tongue, the snake closed his hood, lowered his head to the ground and, turning, made off up the opposite slope. Without taking my eyes off him I groped with my hand on the hill-side and picked up a stone that filled my hand as comfortably as a cricket ball. The snake had just reached a sharp ridge of hard clay when the stone, launched with the utmost energy I was capable of, struck it on the back of the head. The blow would have killed any other snake outright, but the only, and very alarming, effect it had on the hamadryad was to make it whip round and come straight towards me. A second and a larger stone fortunately caught it on the neck when it had covered half the distance between us, and after that the rest was easy. With a great feeling of satisfaction I completed the second circle round the village, and though it proved as fruitless as the first, I was elated at having killed the snake. Now, for the first time in many days, I had a feeling that my search for the man-eater would be successful.

The following day I again searched the forest surrounding the village, and towards evening found the fresh pug-marks of the tiger at the edge of a ploughed field overlooking the village. The occupants of the village, numbering about a hundred, were by now thoroughly alarmed, and leaving them with the assurance that I would return early next day, I set out on my lonely four-mile walk back to the Forest Bungalow.

To walk with safety through forests or along deserted roads in an area in which a man-eater is operating calls for the utmost caution and the strict observance of many rules. It is only when the hunter has repeatedly been the hunted that the senses can be attuned to the 'required pitch, and those rules be strictly adhered to, the breaking of which would provide the man-eater with an easy victim.

The reader may ask, 'Why a lonely walk?' when I probably had men and to spare with me in camp. My answer to this very natural question would be: first, because one is apt to get careless and rely too much on one's companions, and second, because in a mix-up with a tiger one has a better chance when one is alone.

The next morning, as I approached the village, I saw an eager throng of men waiting for me, and when within earshot I was greeted with the gratifying news that a buffalo had been killed during the night. The animal had been killed in the village, and after being dragged some distance along the ridge had been taken down into a narrow, deep, and very heavily wooded valley on the north face of the hill.

A very careful reconnaissance from a projecting rock on the ridge satisfied me that an approach down the steep hill, along the line of the drag, would not be advisable, and that the only thing to do was to make a wide detour, enter the valley from the lower end, and work up to the spot where I expected to find the kill.

This manoeuvre was successfully accomplished, and by midday I arrived at the spot – marked from above – where the valley flattened out for a hundred yards before going straight up three hundred yards to the ridge above. It was at the upper end of this flat bit of ground that I expected to find the kill, and with luck, the tiger. The long and difficult climb up the valley through dense thickets of thorn bush and stunted bamboo had brought out a bath of sweat, and as it was not advisable to take on a job where quick firing might be necessary with sweaty hands, I sat down for a much-needed rest and for a smoke.

The ground in front of me was strewn with large smooth boulders among which a tiny stream meandered, forming wherever possible small crystal-clear pools. Shod with the thinnest of rubber-soled shoes, the going over these boulders was ideal for my purpose, and when I had cooled and dried I set off to stalk the kill in the hope of finding the tiger lying asleep near it. When three-quarters of the ground had been covered I caught sight of the kill tucked away under a bank of ferns, and about twenty-five yards away from where the hill went steeply up to the ridge. The tiger was not in sight, and, very cautiously drawing level with the kill, I took up my position on a fiat boulder to scan every inch of ground visible.

The premonition of impending danger is too well known and established a fact to need any comment. For three or four minutes I had stood perfectly still with no thought of danger, and then all at once I became aware that the tiger was looking at me at a very short range. The same sense that had conveyed the feeling of impending danger to me had evidently operated in the same way on the tiger and awakened him from his sleep. To my left front were some dense bushes, growing on a bit of flat ground. On these bushes, distant fifteen to twenty feet from me, and about the same distance from the kill, my interest centred. Presently the bushes were gently stirred and the next second I caught sight of the tiger going at full speed up the steep hill-side. Before I could get the rifle to bear on him he disappeared behind a creeper-covered tree, and it was not until he had covered about sixty yards that I again saw him, as he was springing up the face of a rock. At my shot he fell backwards and came roaring down the hill, bringing an avalanche of stones with him. A broken back, I concluded; and just as I was wondering how best to deal with him when he should arrive all-of-a-heap at my feet, the roaring ceased, and the next minute, as much to my relief as to my disappointment, I saw him going full-out, and apparently unwounded across the side of the hill. The momentary glimpses I caught of him offered no shot worth taking, and with a crash through some dry bamboos he disappeared round the shoulder of the hill into the next valley.

I subsequently found that my bullet, fired at an angle of seventy-five degrees, had hit the tiger on the left elbow and chipped out a section from that bone which some cynical humorist has named the 'funny bone'. Carrying on, the bullet had struck the rock and, splashing back, had delivered a smashing blow on the point of the jaw. Neither wound, however painful it may have been, was fatal, and the only result of my following up the very light blood trail into the next valley was to be growled at from a dense thorn thicket, to enter which would have been suicidal.

My shot had been heard in the village, and an expectant crowd were waiting for me on the ridge. They were even more disappointed, if that were possible, than I was at the failure of my carefully planned and as carefully executed stalk.

On visiting the kill the following morning I was very pleased and not a little surprised to find that the tiger had returned to it during the night and taken a light meal. The only way now of getting a second shot was to sit up over the kill; and here a difficulty presented itself. There were no suitable trees within convenient distance of the kill, and the very unpleasant experience I had had on a former occasion had effectively cured me of sitting at night on the ground for a man-eater. While still undecided where to sit, I heard the tiger call, some distance down the valley up which I had climbed the previous day. The calling of the tiger offered me a very welcome chance of shooting it in the most pleasant way it is possible of bringing one of these animals to bag. The conditions under which a tiger can be called up are (a) when rampaging through the forest in search of a mate, and (h) when lightly wounded. It goes without saying that the sportsman must be able to call sufficiently well to deceive the tiger, and that the call must come from a spot to which the tiger will quite naturally come – a dense thicket or a patch of heavy grass – and that the sportsman must be prepared to take his shot at a very close range. I am quite certain that many sportsmen will be sceptical of the statement I have made that a lightly wounded tiger will come to a call. I would ask all such to reserve their judgement until they have tried the experiment for themselves. On the present occasion, however, though the tiger answered me, call for call, for upwards of an hour, he refused to come any nearer, and I attributed my failure to the fact that I was calling from the spot where the previous day the tiger had met with an unfortunate experience.

    The tree I finally selected was growing on the very edge of a perpendicular bank and had a convenient branch about eight feet from the ground. When sitting on this branch I should be thirty feet from, and directly above, the boulder-strewn ravine up which I expected the tiger to come. The question of the tree settled, I returned to the ridge where I had instructed my men to meet me with breakfast.

By four o'clock in the evening I was comfortably seated on the branch and prepared for a long and a hard sit-up. Before leaving my men I had instructed them to cooee to me from the ridge at sunrise next morning. If l answered with the call of a leopard they were to sit tight, but if they received no answer, they were to form two parties with as many villagers as they could collect and come down on either side of the valley, shouting and throwing stones.

I have acquired the habit of sleeping in any position on a tree, and as I was tired the evening did not pass unpleasantly. As the setting sun was gilding the hill-tops above me I was roused to full consciousness by the alarm-call of a langur. I soon located the monkey, sitting in a tree-top on the far side of the valley, and as it was looking in my direction I concluded it had mistaken me for a leopard. The alarm-call was repeated at short intervals, and finally ceased as darkness came on.

Hour after hour I strained my eyes and ears, and was suddenly startled by a stone rolling down the hill-side and striking my tree. The stone was followed by the stealthy padding of a heavy, soft-footed animal, unmistakably the tiger. At first I comforted myself with the thought that his coming in this direction, instead of up the valley, was accidental, but this thought was soon dispelled when he started to emit low deep growls from immediately behind me. Quite evidently he had come into the valley while I was having breakfast, and, taking up a position on the hill, where the monkey had later seen him, had watched me climbing into the tree. Here was a situation I had not counted on and one that needed careful handling. The branch that had provided a comfortable seat while day-light lasted admitted of little change of position in the dark. I could, of course, have fired off my rifle into the air, but the terrible results I have seen following an attempt to drive away a tiger at very close quarters by discharging a gun dissuaded me from taking this action. Further, even if the tiger had not attacked, the discharge of the rifle (a 450/400) so near him would probably have made him leave the locality and all my toil would have gone for nothing.

I knew the tiger would not spring, for that would have carried him straight down a drop of thirty feet on to the rocks below. But there was no need for him to spring, for by standing on his hind legs he could easily reach me. Lifting the rifle off my lap and reversing it, I pushed the barrel between my left arm and side, depressing the muzzle and slipping up the safety-catch as I did so. This movement was greeted by a deeper growl than any that had preceded it. If the tiger now reached up for me he would in all probability come in contact with the rifle, round the triggers of which my fingers were crooked, and even if I failed to kill him the confusion following on my shot would give me a sporting chance of climbing higher into the tree. Time dragged by on leaden feet, and, eventually tiring of prowling about the hillside and growling, the tiger sprang across a little ravine on my left and a few minutes later I heard the welcome sound of a bone being cracked at the kill. At last I was able to relax in my uncomfortable position and the only sounds I heard for the rest of the night came from the direction of the kill.

The sun had been up but a few minutes and the valley was still in deep shadow when my men cooeed from the ridge, and almost immediately afterwards I caught sight of the tiger making off at a fast canter up, and across, the hill on my left. In the uncertain light and with my night-long-strained eyes the shot was a very difficult one, but I took it, and, had the satisfaction of seeing the bullet going home. Turning with a great roar, he came straight for my tree, and, as he was in the act of springing, the second bullet, with great good fortune, crashed into his chest. Diverted in his spring by the impact of the heavy bullet, the tiger struck the tree just short of me, and ricocheting off it went headlong into the valley below, where his fall was broken by one of the small pools already alluded to. He floundered out of the water, leaving it dyed red with his blood, and went lumbering down the valley and out of sight.

Fifteen hours on the hard branch had cramped every muscle in my body, and it was not until I had swarmed down the tree, staining my clothes in the great gouts of blood the tiger had left on it, and had massaged my stiff limbs, that I was able to follow him. He had gone but a short distance, and I found him lying dead at the foot of a rock in another pool of water.

Contrary to my orders, the men collected on the ridge, hearing my shot and the tiger's roar followed by a second shot, came in a body down the hill. Arrived at the blood-stained tree, at the foot of which my soft hat was lying, they not unnaturally concluded I had been carried off by the tiger. Hearing their shouts of alarm I called out to them, and again they came running down the valley, only to be brought up with a gasp of dismay when they saw my blood-stained clothes. Reassured that I was not injured and that the blood on my clothes was not mine, a moment later they were crowding round the tiger. A stout sapling was soon cut and lashed to it by creepers, and the tiger, with no little difficulty and a great deal of shouting, was carried up the steep hill to the village.

Jim Corbett

COPY OF PETITION BY THE PEOPLE OP GARHWAL

From
The Public of patty Painaun, Bungi and Bickla Badalpur
District Garhwal

To
Captain J. E. Carbitt, Esq., I.A.R.O., Kaladhungi Distt.
Naini Tal

Respected Sir

We all the public (of the above 3 Patties) most humbly and respectfully beg to lay the following few lines for favour of your kind consideration and doing needful.

That in this vicinity a tiger has turned out man-eater since December last. Up to this date he has killed 5 men and wounded 2. So we the public are in a great distress. By the fear of this tiger we cannot watch our wheat crop at night so the deers have nearly ruined it. We cannot go in the forest for fodder grass nor we can enter our catties in the forest to graze so many of our cattle arc to die. Under the circumstances we arc nearly to be ruined. The Forest officials are doing every possible arrangement to kill this tiger but there is no hope of any success. 2 shikari gentlemen also tried to shoot it but unfortunately they could not get it. Our kind District Magistrate has notified Rs. 150 reward for killing this tiger, so every one is trying to kill it but no success. We have heard that your kind self have killed many man-eating tigers and leopards. For this you have earned a good name specially in Kumaon revenue Division. The famous man-eater leopard of Nagpur has been shoot by you. This is the voice of all the public here that this tiger also will be killed only by you. So we the public venture to request that you very kindly take trouble to come to this place and shoot t his tiger (our enemy) and save the public from this calamity. For this act of kindness we the public will be highly obliged and will pray for your long life and prosperity. Hope you will surely consider on our condition and take trouble to come here for saving us from this calamity. The route to this place is as follows Ramnagar to Sultan, Sultan to Lahachaur, Lahachaur to Kanda. If your honour kindly inform us the date of your arrival at Ramnagar we will send our men and cart to Ramnagar to meet you and accompany you.

We beg to remain Sir Your most sincerely

Dated Jharat
The 18th February 1933

Signed Govind Singh Negi
Headman Village Jhara
followed by 40 signatures and 4 thumb impressions of inhabitants of Painaun, Bungi, and Bickla Badalpur Patties.

Address
   The Govind Singh Negi
   Village Jharat Patty
   Painaun, P.O.
   Badialgaon Distt., Garhwal, U.P.

The promise mentioned on page 139 was made after receiving this petition.

In remote areas in which long-established man-eaters are operating, many gallant acts of heroism are performed, which the local inhabitants accept as everyday occurrences and the outside world has no means of hearing about. I should like to put on record one such act concerning the Kanda man-eater's last human victim. I arrived on the scene shortly after the occurrence, and from details supplied by the villagers and from a careful examination of the ground, which had not been disturbed in the interval, I am able to present you with a story which I believe to be correct in every detail.

In the village near which I shot the Kanda man-eater lived an elderly man and his only son. The father had served in the army during the 1914-18 war, and it was his ambition to get his son enlisted in the Royal Garhwal Rifles – not as simple a job in the 'piping days of peace', when vacancies were few and applicants many, as it is to-day. Shortly after the lad's eighteenth birthday a party of men passed through the village on their way to the bazaar at Lansdowne. The lad joined this party, and immediately on arrival at Lansdowne presented himself at the Recruiting Office. As his father had taught him to salute with military precision and how to conduct himself in the presence of a Recruiting Officer, he was accepted without any hesitation, and, after enrolment, was given leave to deposit his few personal possessions at home before starting his army training.

He arrived back home at about midday, after an absence of five days, and was told by the friends who thronged round him to hear his news that his father was away ploughing their small holding at the extreme end of the village and would not return before nightfall. (The field that was being ploughed was the same one on which I had seen the pug-marks of the man-eater the day I killed the hamadryad.)

One of the lad's jobs had been to provide fodder for their cattle, and after he had partaken of the midday meal in a neighbour's house he set out with a party of twenty men to collect leaves.

The village, as I have told you, is situated on a ridge, and is surrounded by forests. Two women had already been killed by the man-eater while cutting grass in these forests, and for several months the cattle had been kept alive on leaves cut from the trees surrounding the village. Each day the men had to go farther afield to get their requirements, and on this particular day the party of twenty-one, after crossing the cultivated land, went for a quarter of a mile down a very steep rocky hill to the head of the valley, which runs east for eight miles, through dense forest, to where it meets the Ramganga River opposite the Dhikala Forest Bungalow.

At the head of the valley the ground is more or less flat and overgrown with big trees. Here the men separated, each climbing into a tree of his choice, and after cutting the quantity of leaves required they tied them into bundles with rope brought for the purpose, and returned to the village in twos and threes.

Either when the party of men were coming down the hill, talking at the tops of their voices to keep up their courage and scare away the man-eater, or when they were on the trees shouting to each other, the tiger, who was lying up in a dense patch of cover half a mile down the valley, heard them. Leaving the cover, in which it had four days previously killed and eaten a sambur hind, the tiger crossed a stream and by way of a cattle-track that runs the entire length of the valley hurried up in the direction of the men.

(The speed at which a tiger has travelled over any ground on which he has left signs of his passage can be easily determined from the relative position of his fore and hind pug-marks.)

The lad of my story had selected a Bauhinea-tree from which to cut leaves for his cattle. This tree was about twenty yards above the cattle-track, and the upper branches were leaning out over a small ravine in which there were two big rocks. From a bend in the cattle-track the tiger saw the lad on the tree, and after lying down and watching him for some time it left the track and concealed itself behind a fallen silk cotton-tree some thirty yards from the ravine. When the lad had cut all the leaves he needed he descended from the tree and collected them in a heap, preparatory to tying them into a bundle. While doing this on the open fl.at ground he was comparatively safe, but unfortunately he had noticed that two of the branches he had cut had fallen into the ravine between the two big rocks, and he sealed his fate by stepping down into the ravine to recover them. As soon as he was out of sight the tiger left the shelter of the fallen tree and crept forward to the edge of the ravine, and as the lad was stooping down to pick up the branches, it sprang on him and killed him. Whether the killing took place while the other men were still in the trees or after they had left, it was not possible for me to determine.

The father of the lad returned to the village at sunset and was greeted with the very gratifying news that his son had been accepted for the army, and that he had returned from Lansdowne on short leave. Asking where the lad was, he was told that he had gone out earlier in the day to get fodder, and surprise was expressed that the father had not found him at home. After bedding down the bullocks, the father went from house to house to find his son. All the men who had been out that day were questioned in turn, and all had the same tale to tell – that they had separated at the head of the valley, and no one could remember having seen the lad after that.

Crossing the terraced cultivated land, the father went to the edge of the steep hill, and called and called again to his son, but received no answer.

Night was by now setting in. The man returned to his home and lit a small, smoke-dimmed lantern, and as he passed through the village he horrified his neighbours by telling them, in reply to their questions, that he was going to look for his son. He was asked if he had forgotten the man-eater, and answered that it was because of the man-eater that he was so anxious to find his son, for it was possible he had fallen off a tree and injured himself and, for fear of attracting the man-eater, had not answered to his call.

He did not ask anyone to accompany him, and no one offered to do so, and for the whole of that night he searched up and down that valley in which no one had dared to set foot since the advent of the man-eater. Four times during the night – as I saw from his footprints – when going along the cattle-track he had passed within ten feet of where the tiger was lying eating his son.

Weary and heartsick he climbed a little way up the rocky hill as light was coming, and sat down for a rest. From this raised position he could see into the ravine. At sunrise he saw a glint of blood on the two big rocks, and hurrying down to the spot he found all that the tiger had left of his son. These remains he collected and took back to his home, and when a suitable shroud had been procured, his friends helped him to carry the remains to the burning ghat on the banks of the Mandal River.

I do not think it would be correct to assume that acts such as these are performed by individuals who lack imagination and who therefore do not realize the grave risks they run. The people of our hills, in addition to being very sensitive to their environments, are very superstitious, and every hill-top, valley, and gorge is credited with possessing a spirit in one form or another, all of the evil and malignant kind most to be feared during the hours of darkness. A man brought up in these surroundings, and menaced for over a year by a man-eater, who, unarmed and alone, from sunset to sunrise, could walk through dense forests which his imagination peopled with evil spirits, and in which he had every reason to believe a man-eater was lurking, was in my opinion possessed of a quality and a degree of courage that is given to few. All the more do I give him credit for his act of heroism for not being conscious that he had done anything unusual or worthy of notice. When at my request he sat down near the man-eater to enable me to take a photograph, he looked up at me and said, in a quiet and collected voice, 'I am content now, sahib, for you have avenged my son.'

This was the last of the three man-eaters that I had promised the District Officials of Kumaon, and later the people of Garhwal, that I would do my best to rid them of.

THE PIPAL PAM TIGER

Beyond the fact that he was born in a ravine running deep into the foot-hills and was one of a family of three, I know nothing of his early history.

He was about a year old when, attracted, by the calling of a chital hind early one November morning, I found h pug-marks in the sandy bed of a little stream known locally as Pipal Pani. I thought at first that he had strayed from his mother's care, but, as week succeeded week and his single tracks showed on the game-paths of the forest, I came to the conclusion that the near approach of the breeding season was an all-sufficient reason for his being alone. Jealously guarded one day, protected at the cost of the parent life if necessary, and set adrift the next is the lot of all jungle folk; nature's method of preventing inbreeding.

That winter he lived on pea-fowl, kakar, small pig, and an occasional chital hind, making his home in a prostrate giant of the forest felled for no apparent reason, and hollowed out by time an<l porcupines. Here he brought most of his kills, basking, when the days were cold, on the smooth bole of the tree, where many a leopard had basked before him.

It was not until January was well advanced that I saw the cub at close quarters. I was out one evening without any definite object in view, when I saw a crow rise from the ground and wipe its beak as it lit on the branch of a tree. Crows, vultures, and magpies always interest me in the jungle, and many are the kills I have found, both in India and in Africa, with the help of these birds. On the present occasion the crow led me to the scene of an overnight tragedy. A chital had been killed and partly eaten and, attracted to the spot probably as I had been, a party of men passing along the road, distant some fifty yards, had cut up and removed the remains. All that was left of the chital were a few splinters of bone and a little congealed blood off which the crow had lately made his meal. The absence of thick cover and the proximity of the road convinced me that the animal responsible for the kill ha<l not witnessed the removal and that it would return in due course; so I decided to sit up, and made myself as comfortable in a plum-tree as the thorns permitted.

I make no apology to you, my reader, if you differ with me on the ethics of the much-debated subject of sitting up over kills. Some of my most pleasant shikar memories centre round the hour or two before sunset that I have spent in a tree over a natural kill, ranging from the time when, armed with a muzzle-loader whipped round with brass wire to prevent the cracked barrel from bursting, I sat over a langur killed by a leopard, to a few days ago, when with the most modern rifle across my knees, I watched a tigress and her two full-grown cubs eat up the sambur stag they had killed, and counted myself no poorer for not having secured a trophy.

True, on the present occasion there is no kill below me, but, for the reasons given, that will not affect my chance of a shot; scent to interest the jungle folk there is in plenty in the blood-soaked ground, as witness the old grey-whiskered boar who has been quietly rooting along for the past ten minutes, and who suddenly stiffens to attention as

Jim Corbett

he comes into the line of the blood-tainted wind. His snout held high, and worked as only a pig can work that member, tells him more than I was able to glean from the ground, which showed no tracks; his method of approach, a short excursion to the right and back into the wind, and then a short excursion to the left and again back into the wind, each manoeuvre bringing him a few yards nearer, indicates the chital was killed by a tiger. Making sure once and again that nothing worth eating has been left, he finally trots off and disappears from view.

Two chital, both with horns in velvet, now appear, and from the fact that they are coming down-wind, and making straight for the blood-soaked spot, it is evident they were witnesses to the overnight tragedy. Alternately snuffing the ground or standing rigid with every muscle tensed for instant flight, they satisfy their curiosity and return the way they came.

Curiosity is not a human monopoly: many an animal's life is cut short by indulging in it. A dog leaves the veranda to bark at a shadow, a deer leaves the herd to investigate a tuft of grass that no wind agitated, and the waiting leopard is provided with a meal.

The sun is nearing the winter line when a movement to the right front attracts attention. An animal has crossed an opening between two bushes at the far end of a wedge of scrub that terminates thirty yards from my tree. Presently the bushes at my end part, and out into the open, with never a look to right or left, steps the cub. Straight up to the spot where his kill had been he goes, his look of expectancy giving place to one of disappointment as he realizes that his chital, killed, possibly, after hours of patient stalking, is gone. The splinters of bone and congealed blood are rejected, and his interest centres on a tree-stump lately used as a butcher's block, to which some shreds of flesh are adhering. I was not the only one who carried fire-arms in these jungles and, if the cub was to grow into a tiger, it was necessary he should be taught the danger of carelessly approaching kills in daylight. A scatter-gun and dust-shot would have served my purpose better, but the rifle will have to do this time; and, as he raises his head to smell the stump, my bullet crashes into the hard wood an inch from his nose. Only once in the years that followed did the cub forget that lesson.

The following winter I saw him several times. His ears did not look so big now, and he had changed his baby hair for a coat of rich tawny red with well-defined stripes. The hollow tree had been given up to its rightful owners, a pair of leopards, new quarters found in a thick belt of scrub skirting the foot-hills, and young sambur added to his menu.

On my annual descent from the hills next winter, the familiar pug-marks no longer showed on the game-paths and at the drinking-places, and for several weeks I thought the cub had abandoned his old haunts and gone farther afield. Then one morning his absence was explained, for side by side with his tracks were the smaller and more elongated tracks of the mate he had gone to find. I only once saw the tigers, for the cub was a tiger now, together. I had been out before dawn to try to bag a serow that lived on the foot-hills, and returning along a fire-track my attention was arrested by a vulture, perched on the dead limb of a sal-tree.

The bird had his back towards me, and was facing a short stretch of scrub with dense jungle beyond. Dew was still heavy on the ground, and without a sound I reached the

tree and peered round. One antler of a dead sambur, for no living deer would lie in that position, projected above the low bushes. A convenient moss-covered rock afforded my rubber-shod feet silent and safe hold, and as I drew myself erect, the sambur came into full view. The hind quarters had been eaten away and, lying on either side of the kill, were the pair, the tiger being on the far side with only his hind legs showing. Both tigers were asleep. Ten feet straight in front, to avoid a dead branch, and thirty feet to the left would give me a shot at the tiger's neck, but in planning the stalk I had forgotten the silent spectator. Where I stood I was invisible to him, but before the ten feet had been covered I came into view and, alarmed at my near proximity, he flapped off his perch, omitting as he did so to notice a thin creeper dependent from a branch above him against which he collided, and came ignominiously to ground. The tigress was up and away in an instant, clearing at a bound the kill, and her mate, the tiger, not being slow to follow; a possible shot, but too risky with thick jungle ahead where a wounded animal would have all the advantages. To those who have never tried it, I can recommend the stalking of leopards and tigers on their kills as a most pleasant form of sport. Great care should however be taken over the shot, for if the animal is not killed outright, or anchored, trouble is bound to follow.

A week later the tiger resumed his bachelor existence. A change had now come over his nature. Hitherto he had not objected to my visiting his kills, but, after his mate left, at the first drag I followed up I was given very clearly to understand that no liberties would in future be permitted. The angry growl of a tiger at close quarters, than which there is no more terrifying sound in the jungles, has to be heard to be appreciated.

Early in March the tiger killed his first full-grown buffalo. I was near the foot-hills one evening when the agonized bellowing of a buffalo, mingled with the angry roar of a tiger, rang through the forest. I located the sound as coming from a ravine about six hundred yards away. The going was bad, mostly over loose rocks and through thorn bushes, and when I crawled up a steep bluff commanding a view of the ravine the buffalo's struggles were over, and the tiger was nowhere to be seen. For an hour I lay with finger on trigger without seeing anything of the tiger. At dawn next morning I again crawled up the bluff, to find the buffalo lying just as I had left her. The soft ground, torn up by hoof and claw, testified to the desperate nature of the struggle, and it was not until the buffalo had been hamstrung that the tiger had finally succeeded in pulling her down, in a fight which had lasted from ten to fifteen minutes. The tiger's tracks led across the ravine and, on following them up, I found a Jong smear of blood on a rock, and, a hundred yards farther on, another smear on a fallen tree. The wound inflicted by the buffalo's horns was in the tiger's head and sufficiently severe to make the tiger lose all interest in the kill, for he never returned to it.

Three years later the tiger, disregarding the lesson received when a cub (his excuse may have been that it was the close season for tigers), incautiously returned to a kill, over which a zamindar and some of his tenants were sitting at night, and received a bullet in the shoulder which fractured the bone. No attempt was made to follow him up, and thirty-six hours later, his shoulder covered with a swarm of flies, he limped through the compound of the Inspection Bungalow, crossed a bridge flanked on the far side by a double row of tenanted houses, the occupants of which stood at their doors to watch him pass, entered the gate of a walled-in compound and took possession of a vacant godown. Twenty-four hours later, possibly alarmed by the number of people who had collected from neighbouring villages to see him, he left the compound the way he had entered it, passed our gate, and made his way to the lower end of our village. A bullock belonging to one of our tenants had died the previous night and had been dragged into some bushes at the edge of the village; this the tiger found, and here he remained a few days, quenching his thirst at an irrigation furrow.

When we came down from the hills two months later the tiger was living on small animals (calves, sheep, goats, etc.) that he was able to catch on the outskirts of the village. By March his wound had healed, leaving his right foot turned inwards. Returning to the forest where he had been wounded, he levied heavy toll on the village cattle, taking, for safety's sake, but one meal off each, and in this way killing five times as many as he would ordinarily have done. The zamindar who had wounded him and who had a herd of some four hundred head of cows and buffaloes was the chief sufferer.

In the succeeding years he gained as much in size as in reputation, and many were the attempts made by sportsmen, and others, to bag him.

One November evening, a villager, armed with a single-barrel, muzzle-loading gun, set out to try to bag a pig, selecting for his ground machan an isolated bush growing in a twenty-yard-wide *rowkah* (dry watercourse) running down the centre of some broken ground. This ground was rectangular, flanked on the long sides by cultivated land

and on the short sides by a road and by a ten-foot canal that formed the boundary between our cultivation and the forest. In front of the man was a four-foot-high bank with a cattle-track running along the upper edge; behind him a patch of dense scrub. At 8 p.m. an animal appeared on the track and, taking what aim he could, he fired. On receiving the shot the animal fell off the bank, and passed with a few feet of the man, grunting as it entered the scrub behind. Casting aside his blanket, the man ran to his hut two hundred yards away. Neighbours soon collected and, on hearing the man's account, came to the conclusion that a pig had been hard hit. It would be a pity, they said, to leave the pig for hyenas and jackals to eat, so a lantern was lit and as a party of six bold spirits set out to retrieve the bag, one of my tenants (who declined to join the expedition, and who confessed to me later that he had no stomach for looking for wounded pig in dense scrub in the dark) suggested that the gun should be loaded and taken.

His suggestion was accepted and, as a liberal charge of powder was being rammed home, the wooden ramrod jammed and broke inside the barrel. A trivial accident which undoubtedly saved the lives of six men. The broken rod was eventually and after great trouble extracted, the gun loaded, and the party set off.

Arrived at the spot where the animal had entered the bushes, a careful search was made and, on blood being found, every effort to find the 'pig' was made; it was not until the whole area had been combed out that the quest for that night was finally abandoned. Early next morning the search was resumed, with the addition of my informant of weak stomach, who was a better woodsman than his companions and who, examining the ground under a bush where there was a lot of blood, collected and brought some bloodstained hairs to me, which I recognized as tiger's hairs. A brother sportsman was with me for the day, and together we went to have a look at the ground.

The reconstruction of jungle events from signs on the ground has always held great interest for me. True, one's deductions are sometimes wrong, but they are also sometimes right. In the present instance I was right in placing the wound in the inner forearm of the right foreleg, but was wrong in assuming the leg had been broken and that the tiger was a young animal and a stranger to the locality.

There was no blood beyond the point where the hairs had been found and, as tracking on the hard ground was impossible, I crossed the canal to where the cattle-track ran through a bed of sand. Here from the pug-marks I found that the wounded animal was not a young tiger as I had assumed, but my old friend the Pipal Pani tiger, who, when taking a short cut through the village, had in the dark been mistaken for a pig.

Once before when badly wounded he had passed through the settlement without harming man or beast, but he was older now, and if driven by pain and hunger might do considerable damage. A disconcerting prospect, for the locality was thickly populated, and I was due to leave within the week, to keep an engagement that could not be put off.

For three days I searched every bit of the jungle between the canal and the foot-hills, an area of about four square miles, without finding any trace of the tiger. On the fourth afternoon, as I was setting out to continue the search, I met an old woman and her son hurriedly leaving the jungle. From them I learnt that the tiger was calling near the foot-hills and that all the cattle in the jungle had stampeded. When out with a rifle I invariably go alone, it is safer in a mix-up, and one can get through the jungle more silently.

However, I stretched a point on this occasion, and let the boy accompany me, since he was very keen on showing me where he had heard the tiger.

Arrived at the foot-hills, the boy pointed to a dense bit of cover, bounded on the far side by the fire-track to which I have already referred, and on the near side by the Pipal Pani stream. Running parallel to and about a hundred yards from the stream was a shallow depression some twenty feet wide, more or less open on my side and fringed with bushes on the side nearer the stream. A well-used path crossed the depression at right angles. Twenty yards from the path, and on the open side of the depression, was a small tree. If the tiger came down the path he would in all likelihood stand for a shot on clearing the bushes. Here I decided to take my stand and, putting the boy into the tree with his feet on a level with my head and instructing him to signal with his toes if from his raised position he saw the tiger before I did, I put my back to the tree and called.

You who have spent as many years in the jungle as I have need no description of the call of a tigress in search of a mate, and to you less fortunate ones I can only say that the call, to acquire which necessitates close observation and the liberal use of throat salve, cannot be described in words.

To my great relief, for I had crawled through the jungle for three days with finger on trigger, I was immediately answered from a distance of about five hundred yards, and for half an hour thereafter – it may have been less and certainly appeared more – the call was tossed back and forth. On the one side the urgent summons of the king, and on the other, the subdued and coaxing answer of his handmaiden. Twice the boy signalled, but I had as yet seen nothing of the tiger, and it was not until the setting sun was flooding the forest with golden light that he suddenly appeared, coming down the path at a fast walk with never a pause as he cleared the bushes. When half-way across the depression, and just as I was raising the rifle, he turned to the right and came straight towards me.

This manoeuvre, unforeseen when selecting my stand, brought him nearer than I had intended he should come and, moreover, presented me with a head shot which at that short range I was not prepared to take. Resorting to an old device, learned long years ago and successfully used on similar occasions, the tiger was brought to a stand without being alarmed. With one paw poised, he slowly raised his head, exposing as he did so his chest and throat. After the impact of the heavy bullet, he struggled to his feet and tore blindly through the forest, coming down with a crash within a few yards of where, attracted by the calling of a chital hind one November morning, I had first seen his pug-marks.

It was only then that I found he had been shot under a misapprehension, for the wound which I feared might make him dangerous proved on examination to be almost healed and caused by a pellet of lead having severed a small vein in his right forearm.

Pleasure at having secured a magnificent trophy – he measured 10 feet 3 inches over curves, and his winter coat was in perfect condition – was not unmixed with regret, for never again would the jungle folk and I listen with held breath to his deep-throated call resounding through the foot-hills, and never again would his familiar pug-marks show on the game-paths that he and I had trodden for fifteen years.

THE THAK
MAN-EATER

Peace had reigned in the Ladhya valley for many months when in September '38 a report was received in Naini Tal that a girl, twelve years of age, had been killed by a tiger at Kot Kindri village. The report, which reached me through Donald Stewart, of the Forest Department, gave no details, and it was not until I visited the village some weeks later that I was able to get particulars of the tragedy. It appeared that, about noon one day, this girl was picking up windfalls from a mango-tree close to and in full view of the village, when a tiger suddenly appeared. Before the men working near by were able to render any assistance, it carried her off. No attempt was made to follow up the tiger, and as all signs of drag and blood trail had been obliterated and washed away long before I arrived on the scene, I was unable to find the place where the tiger had taken the body to.

Kot Kindri is about four miles south-west of Chuka, and three miles due west of Thak. It was in the valley between Kot Kindri and Thak that the Chuka man-eater had been shot the previous April.

During the summer of '38 the Forest Department had marked all the trees in this area for felling, and it was feared that if the man-eater was not accounted for before November – when the felling of the forest was due to start – the contractors would not be able to secure labour, and would repudiate their contracts. It was in this connexion that Donald Stewart had written to me shortly after the girl had been killed, and when in compliance with his request I promised to go to Kot Kindri, I must confess that it was more in the interests of the local inhabitants than in the interests of the contractors that I gave my promise.

My most direct route to Kot Kindri was to go by rail to Tanakpur, and from there by foot via Kaldhunga and Chuka. This route, however, though it would save me a hundred miles of walking, would necessitate my passing through the most deadly malaria belt in northern India, and to avoid it I decided to go through the hills to Mornaula, and from there along the abandoned Sherring road to its termination on the ridge above Kot Kindri.

While my preparations for this long trek were still under way a second report reached Naini Tal of a kill at Sem, a small village on the left bank of the Ladhya and distant about half a mile from Chuka.

The victim on this occasion was an elderly woman, the mother of the Headman of Sem. This unfortunate woman had been killed while cutting brushwood on a steep bank between two terraced fields. She had started work at the farther end of the fifty-yard-long bank, and had cut the brushwood to within a yard of her hut when the tiger sprang on her from the field above. So sudden and unexpected was the attack that the woman only had time to scream once before the tiger killed her, and taking her up the twelve-foot-high bank crossed the upper field and disappeared with her into the dense jungle beyond. Her son, a lad some twenty years of age, was at the time working in a paddy field a few yards away and witnessed the whole occurrence, but was too frightened to try to render any assistance. In response to the lad's urgent summons the Patwari arrived at Sem two days later, accompanied by eighty men he had collected. Following up in the direction the tiger had gone, he found the woman's clothes and a few small bits of bone. This kill had taken place at 2 p.m. on a bright sunny day, and the tiger had eaten its victim only sixty yards from the hut where it had killed her.

On receipt of this second report, Ibbotson, Deputy Commissioner of the three Districts of Almora, Naini Tal, and Garhwal, and I held a council of war, the upshot of which was that Ibbotson, who was on the point of setting out to settle a land dispute at Askot on the border of Tibet, changed his tour programme and, instead of going via Bagashwar, decided to accompany me to Sem, and from there go on to Askot.

The route I had selected entailed a considerable amount of hill-climbing, so we eventually decided to go up the Nandhour valley, cross the watershed between the Nandhour and Ladhya, and follow the latter river down to Sem. The lbbotsons accordingly left Naini Tal on 12 October, and the following day I joined them at Chaurgallia.

Going up the Nandhour and fishing as we went – our best day's catch on light trout rods was a hundred and twenty fish – we arrived on the fifth day at Durga Pepal. Here we left the river, and after a very stiff climb camped for the night on the watershed. Making an early start next morning, we pitched our tents that night on the left bank of the Ladhya, twelve miles from Chalti.

The monsoon had given over early, which was very fortunate for us, for owing to the rock cliffs that run sheer down into the valley, the river has to be crossed every quarter of a mile or so. At one of these fords my cook, who stands five feet in his boots, was washed away and only saved from a watery grave by the prompt assistance of the man who was carrying our lunch basket.

On the tenth day after leaving Chaurgallia we made camp on a deserted field at Sem, two hundred yards from the hut where the woman had been killed, and a hundred yards from the junction of the Ladhya and Sarda Rivers.

Gill Waddell, of the Police, whom we met on our way down the Ladhya, had camped for several days at Sem and had tied out a buffalo that MacDonald of the Forest Department had very kindly placed at our disposal; and though the tiger had visited Sem several times during Waddell's stay, it had not killed the buffalo.

The day following our arrival at Sem, while Ibbotson was interviewing Patwaris, Forest Guards, and Headmen of the surrounding villages, I went out to look for pug-marks. Between our camp and the junction, and also on both banks of the Ladhya, there were long stretches of sand. On this sand I found the tracks of a tigress and of a young male tiger – possibly one of the cubs I had seen in April. The tigress had crossed and re-crossed the Ladhya a number of times during the last few days, and the previous night had walked along the strip of sand in front of our tents. It was this tigress the villagers suspected of being the man-eater, and as she had visited Sem repeatedly since the day the Headman's mother had been killed they were probably correct.

An examination of the pug-marks of the tigress showed her as being an average-sized animal, in the prime of life. Why she had become a man-eater would have to be determined later, but one of the reasons might have been that she had assisted to cat the victims of the Chuka tiger when they were together the previous mating season, and having acquired a taste for human flesh and no longer having a mate to provide her with it, had now turned a man-eater herself. This was only a surmise, and proved later to be incorrect.

Before leaving Naini Tal I had written to the Tahsildar of Tanakpur and asked him to purchase four young male buffaloes for me, and to send them to Sem. One of these buffaloes died on the road, the other three arrived on the 24th, and we tied them out the same evening, together with the one MacDonald had given us. On going out to visit these animals next morning I found the people of Chuka in a great state of excitement. The fields round the village had been recently ploughed, and the previous night the tigress had passed close to three families who were sleeping out on the fields with their cattle; fortunately in each case the cattle had seen the tigress and warned the sleepers of her approach. After leaving the cultivated land the tigress had gone up the track in the direction of Kot Kindri, and had passed close to two of our buffaloes without touching either of them.

The Patwari, Forest Guards, and villagers had told us on our arrival at Sem that it would be a waste of time tying out our young buffaloes, as they were convinced the man-eater would not kill them. The reason they gave was that this method of trying to shoot the man-eater had been tried by others without success, and that in any case if the tigress wanted to eat buffaloes there were many grazing in the jungles for her to choose from. In spite of this advice, however, we continued to tie out our buffaloes, and for the next two nights the tigress passed close to one or more of them, without touching them.

On the morning of the 27th, just as we were finishing

breakfast, a party of men led by Tewari, the brother of the Headman of Thak, arrived in camp and reported that a man of their village was missing. They stated that this man had left the village at about noon the previous day, telling his wife before leaving that he was going to see that his cattle did not stray beyond the village boundary, and as he had not returned they feared he had been killed by the man-eater.

Our preparations were soon made, and at ten o'clock the Ibbotsons and I set off for Thak, accompanied by Tewari and the men he had brought with him. The distance was only about two miles, but the climb was considerable, and as we did not want to lose more time than we could possibly help, we arrived at the outskirts of the village out of breath and in a lather of sweat.

As we approached the village over the scrub-covered flat bit of ground which I have reason to refer to later, we heard a woman crying. The wailing of an Indian woman mourning her dead is unmistakable, and on emerging from the jungle we came on the mourner – the wife of the missing man – and some ten or fifteen men, who were waiting for us on the edge of the cultivated land. These people informed us that from their houses above they had seen some white object, which looked like part of the missing man's clothing, in a field over-grown with scrub thirty yards from where we were now standing. Ibbotson, Tewari, and I set off to investigate the white object, while Mrs Ibbotson took the woman and the rest of the men up to the village.

The field, which had been out of cultivation for some years, was covered with a dense growth of scrub not unlike chrysanthemum, and it was not until we were standing right over the white object that Tewari recognized it as the loincloth of the missing man. Near it was the man's cap.

A struggle had taken place at this spot, but there was no blood. The absence of blood where the attack had taken place and for some considerable distance along the drag could be accounted for by the tigress's having retained her first hold, for no blood would flow in such a case until the hold had been changed.

Thirty yards on the hill above us there was a clump of bushes roofed over with creepers. This spot would have to be looked at before following up the drag, for it was not advisable to have the tigress behind us. In the soft earth under the bushes we found the pug-marks of the tigress, and where she had lain before going forward to attack the man.

Returning to our starting point, we agreed on the following plan of action. Our primary object was to try to stalk the tigress and shoot her on her kill: to achieve this end I was to follow the trail and at the same time keep a look-out in front, with Tewari – who was unarmed – a yard behind me keeping a sharp look-out to right and left, and Ibbotson a yard behind Tewari to safeguard us against an attack from the rear. In the event of either Ibbotson or I seeing so much as a hair of the tigress, we were to risk a shot.

Cattle had grazed over this area the previous day, disturbing the ground, and as there was no blood and the only indication of the tigress's passage was an occasional turned-up leaf or crushed blade of grass, progress was slow. After carrying the man for two hundred yards the tigress had killed and left him, and had returned and carried him off several hours later, when the people of Thak had heard several sambur calling in this direction. The reason for the tigress's not having carried the man away after she had killed him was possibly because his cattle may have witnessed the attack on him, and driven her away.

A big pool of blood had formed where the man had been lying, and as the blood from the wound in his throat had stopped flowing by the time the tigress had picked him up again, and further, as she was now holding him by the small of the back, whereas she had previously held him by the neck, tracking became even more difficult. The tigress kept to the contour of the hill, and as the under-growth here was very dense and visibility only extended to a few yards, our advance was slowed down. In two hours we covered half a mile, and reached a ridge beyond which lay the valley in which, six months previously, we had tracked down and killed the Chuka man-eater. On this ridge was a great slab of rock, which sloped upwards and away from the direction in which we had come. The tigress's tracks went down to the right of the rock, and I felt sure she was lying up under the overhanging portion of it, or in the close vicinity.

Both Ibbotson and I had on light rubber-soled shoes – Tewari was bare-footed – and we had reached the rock without making a sound. Signing to my two companions to stand still and keep a careful watch all round, I got a foothold on the rock, and inch by inch went forward. Beyond the rock was a short stretch of flat ground, and as more of this ground came into view, I felt certain my suspicion that the tigress was lying under the projection was correct. I had still a foot or two to go before I could look over, when I saw a movement to my left front. A golden-rod that had been pressed down had sprung erect, and a second later there was a slight movement in the bushes beyond, and a monkey in a tree on the far side of the bushes started calling.

The tigress had chosen the spot for her after-dinner sleep with great care, but unfortunately for us she was not asleep;

and when she saw the top of my head – I had removed my hat – appearing over the rock, she had risen and, taking a step sideways, had disappeared under a tangle of blackberry bushes. Had she been lying anywhere but where she was she could not have got away, no matter how quickly she had moved, without my getting a shot at her. Our so-carefully-carried-out stalk had failed at the very last moment, and there was nothing to be done now but find the kill, and see if there was sufficient of it left for us to sit up over. To have followed her into the blackberry thicket would have been useless, and would also have reduced our chance of getting a shot at her later.

The tigress had eaten her meal close to where she had been lying, and as this spot was open to the sky and to the keen eyes of vultures she had removed the kill to a place of safety where it would not be visible from the air. Tracking now was easy, for there was a blood trail to follow. The trail led over a ridge of great rocks, and fifty yards beyond these rocks we found the kill.

I am not going to harrow your feelings by attempting to describe that poor torn and mangled thing; stripped of every stitch of clothing and atom of dignity, which only a few hours previously had been a man, the father of two children and the breadwinner of that wailing woman who was facing – without any illusions – the fate of a widow of India. I have seen many similar sights, each more terrible than the one preceding it, in the thirty-two years I have been hunting man-eaters, and on each occasion I have felt that it would have been better to have left the victim to the slayer than recover a mangled mass of flesh to be a nightmare ever after to those who saw it. And yet the cry of blood for blood, and the burning desire to rid a countryside of a menace than which there is none more terrible, is irresistible; and then there is always the hope, no matter how absurd one knows it to be, that the victim by some miracle may still be alive and in need of succour.

The chance of shooting – over a kill – an animal that has in all probability become a man-eater through a wound received over a kill is very remote, and each succeeding failure, no matter what its cause, tends to make the animal more cautious, until it reaches a state when it either abandons its kill after one meal or approaches it as silently and as slowly as a shadow, scanning every leaf and twig with the certainty of discovering its would-be slayer, no matter how carefully he may be concealed or how silent and motionless he may be; a one in a million chance of getting a shot, and yet, who is there among us who would not take it?

The thicket into which the tigress had retired was roughly forty yards square, and she could not leave it without the monkey's seeing her and warning us, so we sat down back to back, to have a smoke and listen if the jungle had anything further to tell us while we considered our next move.

To make a machan it was necessary to return to the village, and during our absence the tigress was almost certain to carry away the kill. It had been difficult to track her when she was carrying a whole human being, but now, when her burden was considerably lighter and she had been disturbed, she would probably go for miles and we might never find her kill again, so it was necessary for one of us to remain on the spot, while the other two went back to the village for ropes.

Ibbotson, with his usual disregard for danger, elected to go back, and while he and Tewari went down the hill to avoid the difficult ground we had recently come over, I stepped up on to a small tree close to the kill. Four feet above ground the tree divided in two, and by leaning on one half and putting my feet against the other, I was able to maintain a precarious seat which was high enough off the ground to enable me to see the tigress if she approached the kill, and also high enough, if she had any designs on me, to see her before she got to within striking distance.

Ibbotson had been gone fifteen or twenty minutes when I heard a rock tilt forward, and then back. The rock was evidently very delicately poised, and when the tigress had put her weight on it and felt it tilt forward she had removed her foot and let the rock fall back into place.   The sound had come from about twenty yards to my left front, the only direction in which it would have been possible for me to have fired without being knocked out of the tree.

Minutes passed, each pulling my hopes down a little lower from the heights to which they had soared, and then, when tension on my nerves and the weight of the heavy rifle were becoming unbearable, I heard a stick snap at the upper end of the thicket. Here was an example of how a tiger can move through the jungle. From the sound she had made I knew her exact position, had kept my eyes fixed on the spot, and yet she had come, seen me, stayed some time watching me, and then gone away without my having seen a leaf or a blade of grass move.

When tension on nerves is suddenly relaxed, cramped and aching muscles call loudly for ease, and though in this case it only meant the lowering of the rifle on to my knees to take the strain off my shoulders and arms, the movement, small though it was, sent a comforting feeling through the whole of my body. No further sound came from the tigress, and an hour or two later I heard Ibbotson returning.

Of all the men I have been on shikar with, Ibbotson is by far and away the best, for not only has he the heart of a lion, but he thinks of everything, and with it all is the most unselfish man that carries a gun. He had gone to fetch a rope, and he returned with rugs, cushions, more hot tea than ever I could drink, and an ample lunch; and while I sat – on the windward side of the kill – to refresh myself, Ibbotson put a man in a tree forty yards away to distract the tigress's attention, and climbed into a tree overlooking the kill to make a rope machan.

When the machan was ready Ibbotson moved the kill a few feet – a very unpleasant job – and tied it securely to the foot of a sapling to prevent the tigress's carrying it away, for the moon was on the wane and the first two hours of the night at this heavily wooded spot would be pitch dark. After a final smoke I climbed on to the machan, and when I had made myself comfortable Ibbotson recovered the man who was making a diversion and set off in the direction of Thak to pick up Mrs Ibbotson and return to camp at Sem.

The retreating party were out of sight, but were not yet out of sound when I heard a heavy body brushing against leaves, and at the same moment the monkey, which had been silent all this time and which I could now see sitting in a tree on the far side of the blackberry thicket, started calling. Here was more luck than I had hoped for, and our ruse of putting a man up a tree to cause a diversion appeared to be working as successfully as it had done on a previous occasion. A tense minute passed, a second, and a third, and then from the ridge where I had climbed on to the big slab of rock a kakar came dashing down towards me, barking hysterically. The tigress was not coming to the kill but had gone off after Ibbotson. I was now in a fever of anxiety, for it was quite evident that she had abandoned her kill and gone to try to secure another victim.

Before leaving, Ibbotson had promised to take every precaution, but on hearing the kakar barking on my side of the ridge he would naturally assume the tigress was moving in the vicinity of the kill, and if he relaxed his precautions the tigress would get her chance. Ten very uneasy minutes for me passed, and then I heard a second kakar barking in the direction of Thak; the tigress was still following, but the ground there was more open, and there was less fear of her attacking the party. The danger to the lbbotsons was, however, not over by any means, for they had to go through two miles of very heavy jungle to reach camp; and if they stayed at Thak until sundown listening for my shot, which I feared they would do and which as a matter of fact they did do, they would run a very grave risk on the way down. Ibbotson fortunately realized the danger and kept his party close together, and though the tigress followed them the whole way – as her pug-marks the following morning showed – they got back to camp safely.

The calling of kakar and sambur enabled me to follow the movements of the tigress. An hour after sunset she was down at the bottom of the valley two miles away. She had the whole night before her, and though there was only one chance in a million of her returning to the kill, I determined not to lose that chance. Wrapping a rug round me, for it was a bitterly cold night, I made myself comfortable in a position in which I could remain for hours without movement.

I had taken my seat on the machan at 4 p.m., and at 10 p.m. I heard two animals coming down the hill towards me. It was too dark under the trees to see them, but when they got to the lee of the kill I knew they were porcupines. Rattling their quills, and making the peculiar booming noise that only a porcupine can make, they approached the kill and, after walking round it several times, continued on their way. An hour later, and when the moon had been up some time, I heard an animal in the valley below. It was moving from east to west, and when it came into the wind blowing downhill from the kill it made a long pause, and then came cautiously up the hill. While it was still some distance away I heard it snuffing the air, and knew it to be a bear. The smell of blood was attracting him, but mingled with it was the less welcome smell of a human being, and taking no chances, he was very carefully stalking the kill. His nose, the keenest of any animal's in the jungle, had apprised him while he was still in the valley that the kill was the property of a tiger. This to a Himalayan bear who fears nothing, and who will, as I have on several occasions seen, drive a tiger away from its kill, was no deterrent, but what was, and what was causing him uneasiness, was the smell of a human being mingled with the smell of blood and tiger.

On reaching the flat ground the bear sat down on his haunches a few yards from the kill, and when he had satisfied himself that the hated human smell held no danger for him he stood erect and turning his head sent a long-drawn-out cry, which I interpreted as a call to a mate, echoing down into the valley. Then without any further hesitation he walked boldly up to the kill, and as he nosed it I aligned the sights of my rifle on him. I know of only one instance of a Himalayan bear eating a human being; on that occasion a woman cutting grass had fallen down a cliff and been killed, and a bear finding the mangled body had carried it away and had eaten it. This bear, however, on

whose shoulder my sights were aligned, appeared to draw the line at human flesh, and after looking at and smelling the kill continued his interrupted course to the west. When the sounds of his retreat died away in the distance the jungle settled down to silence until interrupted, a little after sunrise, by Ibbotson's very welcome arrival.

With Ibbotson came the brother and other relatives of the dead man, who very reverently wrapped the remains in a clean white cloth and, laying it on a cradle made of two saplings and rope which Ibbotson provided, set off for the burning ghat on the banks of the Sarda, repeating under their breath as they went the Hindu hymn of praise 'Ram nam sat hai' with its refrain, 'Satya bol gat hai.'

Fourteen hours in the cold had not been without its effect on me, but after partaking of the hot drink and food Ibbotson had brought, I felt none the worse for my long vigil.

II

After following the Ibbotsons down to Chuka on the evening of the 27th, the tigress, some time during the night, crossed the Ladhya into the scrub jungle at the back of our camp. Through this scrub ran a path that had been regularly used by the villagers of the Ladhya valley until the advent of the man-eater had rendered its passage unsafe. On the 28th the two mail-runners who carried Ibbotson's dak on its first stage to Tanakpur got delayed in camp, and to save time took, or more correctly started to take, a short cut through this scrub. Very fortunately the leading man was on the alert and saw the tigress as she crept through the scrub and lay down near the path ahead of them.

Ibbotson and I had just got back from Thak when these two men dashed into camp, and taking our rifles we hurried off to investigate. We found the pug-marks of the tigress where she had come out on the path and followed the men for a short distance, but we did not see her, though in one place where the scrub was very dense we saw a movement and heard an animal moving off.

On the morning of the 29th, a party of men came down from Thak to report that one of their bullocks had not returned to the cattle-shed the previous night, and on a search being made where it had last been seen a little blood had been found. At 2 p.m. the Ibbotsons and I were at this spot, and a glance at the ground satisfied us that the bullock had been killed and carried away by a tiger. After a hasty lunch Ibbotson and I, with two men following carrying ropes for a machan, set out along the drag. It went diagonally across the face of the hill for a hundred yards and then straight down into the ravine in which I had fired at and missed the big tiger in April. A few hundred yards down this ravine the bullock, which was an enormous animal, had got fixed between two rocks and, not being able to move it, the tiger had eaten a meal off its hind quarters and left it.

The pug-marks of the tiger, owing to the great weight she was carrying, were splayed out, and it was not possible to say whether she was the man-eater or not; but as every tiger in this area was suspect I decided to sit up over the kill. There was only one tree within reasonable distance of the kill, and as the men climbed into it to make a machan the tiger started calling in the valley below. Very hurriedly a few strands of rope were tied between two branches, and while Ibbotson stood on guard with his rifle I climbed the tree and took my seat on what, during the next fourteen hours, proved to be the most uncomfortable as well as the most dangerous machan I have ever sat on. The tree was leaning away from the hill, and from the three uneven strands of rope I was sitting on there was a drop of over a hundred feet into the rocky ravine below.

The tiger called several times as I was getting into the tree and continued to call at longer intervals late into the evening, the last call coming from a ridge half a mile away. It was now quite evident that the tiger had been lying up close to the kill and had seen the men climbing into the tree. Knowing from past experience what this meant, she had duly expressed resentment at being disturbed and then gone away, for though I sat on the three strands of rope until Ibbotson returned next morning, I did not see or hear anything throughout the night.

Vultures were not likely to find the kill, for the ravine was deep and overshadowed by trees, and as the bullock was large enough to provide the tiger with several meals we decided not to sit up over it again where it was now lying, hoping the tiger would remove it to some more convenient place where we should have a better chance of getting a shot. In this, however, we were disappointed, for the tiger did not again return to the kill.

Two nights later the buffalo we had tied out behind our camp at Sem was killed, and through a little want of observation on my part a great opportunity of bagging the man-eater was lost.

The men who brought in the news of this kill reported that the rope securing the animal had been broken, and that the kill had been carried away up the ravine at the lower end of which it had been tied. This was the same ravine in which MacDonald and I had chased a tigress in April, and as on that occasion she had taken her kill some distance up the ravine I now very foolishly concluded she had done the same with this kill.

After breakfast Ibbotson and I went to out find the kill and see what prospect there was for an evening sit-up.

The ravine in which the buffalo had been killed was about fifty yards wide and ran deep into the foot-hills. For two hundred yards the ravine was straight, and then bent round to the left. Just beyond the bend, and on the left-hand side of it, there was a dense patch of young saplings backed by a hundred-foot ridge on which thick grass was growing. In the ravine, and close to the saplings, there was a small pool of water. I had been up the ravine several times in April and had failed to mark the patch of saplings as being a likely place for a tiger to lie up in, and did not take the precautions I should have taken when rounding the bend, with the result that the tigress, who was drinking at the pool, saw us first. There was only one safe line of retreat for her, and she took it. This was straight up the steep hill, over the ridge, and into sal forest beyond.

The hill was too steep for us to climb, so we continued on up the ravine to where a sambur track crossed it, and following this track we gained the ridge. The tigress was now in a triangular patch of jungle bounded by the ridge, the Ladhya, and a cliff down which no animal could go. The area was not large, and there were several deer in it which from time to time advised us of the position of the tigress, but unfortunately the ground was cut up by a number of deep and narrow rain-water channels in which we eventually lost touch with her.

We had not yet seen the kill, so we re-entered the ravine by the sambur track and found the kill hidden among the saplings. These saplings were from six inches to a foot in girth, and were not strong enough to support a platform, so we had to abandon the idea of a machan. With the help of a crowbar, a rock could possibly have been pried from the face of the hill and a place made in which to sit, but this was not advisable when dealing with a man-eater.

Reluctant to give up the chance of a shot, we considered the possibility of concealing ourselves in the grass near the kill, in the hope that the tigress would return before dark and that we should see her before she saw us. There were two objections to this plan: (a) if we did not get a shot and the tigress saw us near her kill she might abandon it, as she had done her other two kills; and (b) between the kill and camp there was very heavy scrub jungle, and if we tried to go through this jungle in the dark the tigress would have us at her mercy. So very reluctantly we decided to leave the kill to the tigress for that night, and hope for the best on the morrow.

On our return next morning we found that the tigress had carried away the kill. For three hundred yards she had gone up the bed of the ravine, stepping from rock to rock, and leaving no drag marks. At this spot – three hundreds yards from where she had picked up the kill – we were at fault, for though there were a number of tracks on a wet patch of ground, none of them had been made while she was carrying the kill. Eventually, after casting round in circles, we found where she had left the ravine and gone up the hill on the left.

This hill up which the tigress had taken her kill was overgrown with ferns and golden-rod and tracking was not difficult, but the going was, for the hill was very steep, and in places a detour had to be made and the track picked up farther on. After a stiff climb of a thousand feet we came to a small plateau, bordered on the left by a cliff a mile wide. On the side of the plateau nearest the cliff the ground was seamed and cracked, and in these cracks a dense growth of sal, two to six feet in height, had sprung up. The tigress had taken her kill into this dense cover, and it was not until we actually trod on it that we were aware of its position.

As we stopped to look at all that remained of the buffalo there was a low growl to our right. With rifles raised we waited for a minute and then, hearing a movement in the undergrowth a little beyond where the growl had come from, we pushed our way through the young sal for ten yards and came on a small clearing, where the tigress had made herself a bed on some soft grass. On the far side of this grass the hill sloped upwards for twenty yards to another plateau, and it was from this slope that the sound we had heard had come. Proceeding up the slope as silently as possible, we had just reached the flat ground, which was about fifty yards wide, when the tigress left the far side and went down into the ravine, disturbing same kaleege pheasants and a kakar as she did so. To have followed her would have been useless, so we went back to the kill and, as there was still a good meal on it, we selected two trees to sit in, and returned to camp.

After an early lunch we went back to the kill and, hampered with our rifles, climbed with some difficulty into the trees we had selected. We sat up for five hours without seeing or hearing anything. At dusk we climbed down from our trees, and stumbling over the cracked and uneven ground eventually reached the ravine when it was quite dark. Both of us had an uneasy feeling that we were being followed, but by keeping close together we reached camp without incident at g p.m.

The lbbotsons had now stayed at Sem as long as it was possible for them to do so, and early next morning they set out on their twelve days' walk to keep their appointment at Askot. Before leaving, Ibbotson extracted a promise from me that I would not follow up any kills alone, or further endanger my life by prolonging my stay at Sem for more than a day or two.

After the departure of the lbbotsons and their fifty men, the camp, which was surrounded by dense scrub, was reduced to my two servants and myself – my coolies were living in a room in the Headman's house – so throughout the day I set all hands to collecting driftwood, of which there was an inexhaustible supply at the junction, to keep a fire going all night. The fire would not scare away the tigress, but it would enable us to see her if she prowled round our tents at night, and anyway the nights were setting in cold and there was ample excuse, if one were needed, for keeping a big fire going all night.

Towards evening, when my men were safely back in camp, I took a rifle and went up the Ladhya to see if the tigress had crossed the river. I found several tracks in the sand, but no fresh ones, and at dusk I returned, convinced that the tigress was still on our side of the river. An hour later, when it was quite dark, a kakar started barking close to our tents and barked persistently for half an hour.

My men had taken over the job of tying out the buffaloes, a task which lbbotson's men had hitherto performed, and next morning I accompanied them when they went out to bring in the buffaloes. Though we covered several miles, I did not find any trace of the tigress. After breakfast I took a rod and went down to the junction, and had one of the best day's fishing I have ever had. The junction was full of big fish, and though my light tackle was broken frequently, I killed sufficient mahseer to feed the camp.

Again, as on the previous evening, I crossed the Ladhya, with the intention of taking up a position on a rock overlooking the open ground on the right bank of the river and watching for the tigress to cross. As I got away from the roar of the water at the junction I heard a sambur and a monkey calling on the hill to my left, and as I neared the rock I came on the fresh tracks of the tigress. Following them back, I found the stones still wet where she had forded the river. A few minutes' delay in camp to dry my fishing-line and have a cup of tea cost a man his life, several thousand men weeks of anxiety, and myself many days of strain, for though I stayed at Sem for another three days I did not get another chance of shooting the tigress.

On the morning of the 7th, as I was breaking camp and preparing to start on my twenty-mile walk to Tanakpur, a big contingent of men from all the surrounding villages arrived and begged me not to leave them to the tender mercies of the man-eater. Giving them what advice it was possible to give people situated as they were, I promised to return as soon as it was possible for me to do so.

I caught the train at Tanakpur next morning and arrived back in Naini Tal on 9 November, having been away nearly a month.

III

I left Sem on 7 November, and on the 12th the tigress killed a man at Thak. I received news of this kill through the Divisional Forest Officer, Haldwani, shortly after we had moved down to our winter home at the foot of the hills, and by doing forced marches I arrived at Chuka a little after sunrise on the 24th.

It had been my intention to breakfast at Chuka and then go on to Thak and make that village my headquarters, but the Headman of Thak, whom I found installed at Chuka, informed me that every man, woman, and child had left Thak immediately after the man had been killed on the 12th, and added that if I carried out my intention of camping at Thak I might be able to safeguard my own life, but it would not be possible to safeguard the lives of my men. This was quite reasonable, and while waiting for my men to arrive, the Headman helped me to select a site for my camp at Chuka, where my men would be reasonably safe and I should have some privacy from the thousands of men who were now arriving to fell the forest.

On receipt of the Divisional Forest Officer's telegram acquainting me of the kill, I had telegraphed to the Tahsildar at Tanakpur to send three young male buffaloes to Chuka. My request had been promptly complied with, and the three animals had arrived the previous evening.

After breakfast I took one of the buffaloes and set out for Thak, intending to tie it up on the spot where the man had been killed on the 12th. The Headman had given me a very graphic account of the events of that date, for he himself had nearly fallen a victim to the tigress. It appeared that towards the afternoon, accompanied by his grand-daughter, a girl ten years of age, he had gone to dig up ginger tubers in a field some sixty yards from his house. This field is about half an acre in extent and is surrounded on three sides by jungle, and being on the slope of a fairly steep hill it is visible from the Headman's house. After the old man and his grand-daughter had been at work for some time, his wife, who was husking rice in the courtyard of the house, called out in a very agitated voice and asked him if he was deaf that he could not hear the pheasants and other birds that were chattering in the jungle above him. Fortunately for him, he acted promptly. Dropping his hoe, he grabbed the child's hand and together they ran back to the house, urged on by the woman who said she could now see a red animal in the bushes at the upper end of the field. Half an hour later the tigress killed a man who was lopping branches off a tree in a field three hundred yards from the Headman's house.

From the description I had received from the Headman I had no difficulty in locating the tree. It was a small gnarled tree growing out of a three-foot-high bank between two terraced fields, and had been lopped year after year for cattle-fodder. The man who had been killed was standing on the trunk holding one branch and cutting another, when the tigress came up from behind, tore his hold from the branch and, after killing him, carried him away into the dense brushwood bordering the fields.

Thak village was a gift from the Chand Rajas, who ruled Kumaon for many hundreds of years before the Gurkha occupation, to the forefathers of the present owners in return for their services at the Punagiri temples. (The promise made by the Chand Rajas that the lands of Thak and two other villages would remain rent-free for all time has been honoured by the British Government for a hundred years.) From a collection of grass huts the village has in the course of time grown into a very prosperous settlement with masonry houses roofed with slate tiles, for not only is the land very fertile, but the revenue from the temples is considerable.

Like all other villages in Kumaon, Thak during its hundreds of years of existence has passed through many vicissitudes, but never before in its long history had it been deserted as it now was. On my previous visits I had found it a hive of industry, but when I went up to it on this afternoon, taking the young buffalo with me, silence reigned over it. Every one of the hundred or more inhabitants had fled, taking their livestock with them – the only animal I saw in the village was a cat, which gave me a warm welcome; so hurried had the evacuation been that many of the doors of the houses had been left wide open. On every path in the village, in the courtyard of the houses, and in the dust before all the doors I found the tigress's pug-marks. The open doorways were a menace, for the path as it wound through the village passed close to them, and in any of the houses the tigress may have been lurking.

On the hill thirty yards above the village were several cattle-shelters, and in the vicinity of these shelters I saw more kaleege pheasants, red jungle fowl, and white-capped babblers than I have ever before seen, and from the confiding way in which they permitted me to walk among them it is quite evident that the people of Thak have a religious prejudice against the taking of life.

From the terraced fields above the cattle-shelters a bird's-eye view of the village is obtained, and it was not difficult, from the description the Headman had given me, to locate the tree where the tigress had secured her last victim. In the soft earth under the tree there were signs of a struggle and a few clots of dried blood. From here the tigress had carried her kill a hundred yards over a ploughed field, through a stout hedge, and into the dense brushwood beyond. The foot-prints from the village and back the way they had come showed that the entire population of the village had visited the scene of the kill, but from the tree to the hedge there was only one track, the track the tigress had made when carrying away her victim. No attempt had been made to follow her up and recover the body.

Scraping away a little earth from under the tree I exposed a root, and to this root I tied my buffalo, bedding it down with a liberal supply of straw taken from a nearby haystack.

The village, which is on the north face of the hill, was now in shadow, and if I was to get back to camp before dark it was time for me to make a start. Skirting round the village to avoid the menace of the open doorways, I joined the path below the houses.

This path after it leaves the village passes under a giant mango-tree from the roots of which issues a cold spring of clear water. After running along a groove cut in a massive slab of rock, this water falls into a rough masonry trough, from where it spreads on to the surrounding ground, rendering it soft and slushy. I had drunk at the spring on my way up, leaving my footprints in this slushy ground, and on approaching the spring now for a second drink, I found the tigress's pug-marks superimposed on my foot-prints. After quenching her thirst the tigress had avoided the path and had gained the village by climbing a steep bank overgrown with strobilanthes and nettles, and taking up a position in the shelter of one of the houses had possibly watched me while I was tying up the buffalo, expecting me to return the way I had gone; it was fortunate for me that I had noted the danger of passing those open doorways a second time, and had taken the longer way round.

When coming up from Chuka I had taken every

precaution to guard against a sudden attack, and it was well that I had done so, for I now found from her pug-marks that the tigress had followed me all the way up from my camp, and next morning when I went back to Thak I found she had followed me from where I had joined the path below the houses, right down to the cultivated land at Chuka.

Reading with the illumination I had brought with me was not possible, so after dinner that night, while sitting near a fire which was as welcome for its warmth as it was for the feeling of security it gave me, I reviewed the whole situation and tried to think out some plan by which it would be possible to circumvent the tigress.

When leaving home on the 22nd I had promised that I would return in ten days, and that this would be my last expedition after man-eaters. Years of exposure and strain and long absences from home – extending as in the case of the Chowgarh tigress and the Rudraprayag leopard to several months on end – were beginning to tell as much on my constitution as on the nerves of those at home, and if by 30 November I had not succeeded in killing this man-eater, others would have to be found who were willing to take on the task.

It was now the night of the 24th, so I had six clear days before me. Judging from the behaviour of the tigress that evening, she appeared to be anxious to secure another human victim, and it should not therefore be difficult for me, in the time at my disposal, to get in touch with her. There were several methods by which this could be accomplished, and each would be tried in turn. The method that offers the greatest chance of success of shooting a tiger in the hills is to sit up in a tree over a kill, and if during that night the tigress did not kill the buffalo I had tied up at Thak, I would the following night, and every night thereafter, tie up the other two buffaloes in places I had already selected, and failing to secure a human kill it was just possible that the tigress might kill one of my buffaloes, as she had done on a previous occasion when the Ibbotsons and I were camped at Sem in April. After making up the fire with logs that would burn all night, I turned in, and went to sleep listening to a kakar barking in the scrub jungle behind my tent.

While breakfast was being prepared the following morning I picked up a rifle and went out to look for tracks on the stretch of sand on the right bank of the river, between Chuka and Sem. The path, after leaving the cultivated land, runs for a short distance through scrub jungle, and here I found the tracks of a big male leopard, possibly the same animal that had alarmed the kakar the previous night. A small male tiger had crossed and re-crossed the Ladhya many times during the past week, and in the same period the man-eater had crossed only once, coming from the direction of Sem. A big bear had traversed the sand a little before my arrival, and when I got back to camp the timber contractors complained that while distributing work that morning they had run into a bear which had taken up a very threatening attitude, in consequence of which their labour had refused to work in the area in which the bear had been seen.

Several thousand men – the contractors put the figure at five thousand – had now concentrated at Chuka and Kumaya Chak to fell and saw up the timber and carry it down to the motor road that was being constructed, and all the time this considerable labour force was working they shouted at the tops of their voices to keep up their courage. The noise in the valley resulting from axe and saw, the crashing of giant trees down the steep hill-side, the breaking of rocks with sledge hammers, and combined with it all the shouting of thousands of men, can better be imagined than described. That there were many and frequent alarms in this nervous community was only natural, and during the next few days I covered much ground and lost much valuable time in investigating false rumours of attacks and kills by the man-eater, for the dread of the tigress was not confined to the Ladhya valley, but extended right down the Sarda through Kaldhunga to the gorge, an area of roughly fifty square miles in which an additional ten thousand men were working.

That a single animal should terrorize a labour force of these dimensions in addition to the residents of the surrounding villages and the hundreds of men who were bringing foodstuffs for the labourers or passing through the valley with hill produce in the way of oranges (purchasable at twelve annas a hundred), walnuts, and chillies to the market at Tanakpur is incredible, and would be unbelievable were it not for the historical, and nearly parallel, case of the man-eaters of Tsavo, where a pair of lions, operating only at night, held up work for long periods on the Uganda Railway.

To return to my story. Breakfast disposed of on the morning of the 25th, I took a second buffalo and set out for Thak. The path, after leaving the cultivated land at Chuka, skirts along the foot of the hill for about half a mile before it divides. One arm goes straight up a ridge to Thak and the other, after continuing along the foot of the hill for another half-mile, zigzags up through Kumaya Chak to Kot Kindri.

At the divide I found the pug-marks of the tigress and followed them all the way back to Thak. The fact that she had come down the hill after me the previous evening was proof that she had not killed the buffalo. This, though very disappointing, was not at all unusual; for tigers will on occasions visit an animal that is tied up for several nights in succession before they finally kill it, for tigers do not kill unless they are hungry.

Leaving the second buffalo at the mango-tree, where there was an abundance of green grass, I skirted round the houses and found No.1 buffalo sleeping peacefully after a big feed and a disturbed night. The tigress, coming from the direction of the village, as her pug-marks showed, had approached to within a few feet of the buffalo, and had then gone back the way she had come. Taking the buffalo down to the spring, I let it graze for an hour or two, and then took it back and tied it up at the same spot where it had been the previous night.

The second buffalo I tied up fifty yards from the mango-tree and at the spot where the wailing woman and villagers had met us the day the Ibbotsons and I had gone up to investigate the human kill. Here a ravine a few feet deep crossed the path, on one side of which there was a dry stump, and on the other an almond-tree in which a machan could be made. I tied No. 2 buffalo to the stump, and bedded it down with sufficient hay to keep it going for several days. There was nothing more to be done at Thak, so I returned to camp and, taking the third buffalo, crossed the Ladhya and tied it up behind Sem, in the ravine where the tigress had killed one of our buffaloes in April.

At my request the Tahsildar of Tanakpur had selected three of the fattest young male buffaloes he could find. All three were now tied up in places frequented by the tigress, and as I set out to visit them on the morning of the 26th I had great hopes that one of them had been killed and that I should get an opportunity of shooting the tigress over it. Starting with the one across the Ladyha, I visited all in turn and found that the tigress had not touched any of them. Again, as on the previous morning, I found her tracks on the path leading to Thak, but on this occasion there was a double set of pug-marks, one coming down and the other going back. On both her journeys the tigress had kept to the path and had passed within a few feet of the buffalo that was tied to the stump, fifty yards from the mango-tree.

On my return to Chuka a deputation of Thak villagers led by the Headman came to my tent and requested me to accompany them to the village to enable them to replenish their supply of foodstuffs, so at midday, followed by the Headman and his tenants, and by four of my own men carrying ropes for a machan and food for me, I returned to Thak and mounted guard while the men hurriedly collected the provisions they needed.

After watering and feeding the two buffaloes I re-tied No. 2 to the stump and took No. 1 half a mile down the hill and tied it to a sapling on the side of the path. I then took the villagers back to Chuka and returned a few hundred yards up the hill for a scratch meal while my men were making the machan.

It was now quite evident that the tigress had no fancy for my fat buffaloes, and as in three days I had seen her tracks five times on the path leading to Thak, I decided to sit up over the path and try to get a shot at her that way. To give me warning of the tigress's approach I tied a goat with a bell round its neck on the path, and at 4 p.m. I climbed into the tree. I told my men to return at 8 a.m. the following morning, and began my watch.

At sunset a cold wind started blowing, and while I was attempting to pull a coat over my shoulders the ropes on one side of the machan slipped, rendering my seat very uncomfortable. An hour later a storm came on, and though it did not rain for long it wet me to the skin, greatly adding to my discomfort. During the sixteen hours I sat in the tree I did not see or hear anything. The men turned up at 8 a.m. I returned to camp for a hot bath and a good meal, and then, accompanied by six of my men, set out for Thak.

The overnight rain had washed all the old tracks off the path, and two hundred yards above the tree I had sat in I found the fresh pug-marks of the tigress, where she had come out of the jungle and gone up the path in the direction of Thak. Very cautiously I stalked the first buffalo, only to find it lying asleep on the path; the tigress had skirted round it, re-joined the path a few yards farther on, and continued up the hill. Following on her tracks, I approached the second buffalo, and as I got near the place where it had been tied two blue Himalayan magpies rose off the ground and went screaming down the hill.

The presence of these birds indicated: (a) that the buffalo was dead, (b) that it had been partly eaten and not carried away, and (c) that the tigress was not in the close vicinity.

On arrival at the stump to which it had been tied I saw that the buffalo had been dragged off the path and partly eaten, and on examining the animal I found it had not been killed by the tigress, but that it had in an probability died of snake-bite (there were many hamadryads in the surrounding jungles), and that, finding it lying dead on the path, the tigress had eaten a meal off it and had then tried to drag it away. When she found she could not break the rope, she had partly covered it over with dry leaves and brushwood and continued on her way up to Thak.

Tigers as a rule are not carrion eaters, but they do on occasions eat animals they themselves have not killed. For instance, on one occasion I left the carcass of a leopard on a fire-track and, when I returned next morning to recover a knife I had forgotten, I found that a tiger had removed the carcass to a distance of a hundred yards and eaten two-thirds of it.

On my way up from Chuka I had dismantled the machan I had sat on the previous night, and while two of my men climbed into the almond-tree to make a seat for me – the tree was not big enough for a machan – the other four went to the spring to fill a kettle and boil some water for tea. By 4 p.m. I had partaken of a light meal of biscuits and tea, which would have to keep me going until next day, and refusing the men's request to be permitted to stay the night in one of the houses in Thak I sent them back to camp. There was a certain amount of risk in doing this, but it was nothing compared to the risk they would run if they spent the night in Thak.

My seat on the tree consisted of several strands of rope tied between two upright branches, with a couple of strands lower down for my feet to rest on. When I had settled down comfortably I pulled the branches round me and secured them in position with a thin cord, leaving a small opening to see and fire through. My 'hide' was soon tested, for shortly after the men had gone the two magpies returned, and attracted others, and nine of them fed on the kill until dusk. The presence of the birds enabled me to get some sleep, for they would have given me warning of the tigress's approach, and with their departure my all-night vigil started.

There was still sufficient daylight to shoot by when the

moon, a day off the full, rose over the Nepal hills behind me and flooded the hill-side with brilliant light. The rain of the previous night had cleared the atmosphere of dust and smoke and, after the moon had been up a few minutes, the light was so good that I was able to see a sambur and her young one feeding in a field of wheat a hundred and fifty yards away.

The dead buffalo was directly in front and about twenty yards away, and the path along which I expected the tigress to come was two or three yards nearer, so I should have an easy shot at a range at which it would be impossible to miss the tigress – provided she came; and there was no reason why she should not do so.

The moon had been up two hours, and the sambur had approached to within fifty yards of my tree, when a kakar started barking on the hill just above the village. The kakar had been barking for some minutes when suddenly a scream, which I can only, very inadequately, describe as 'Ar-Ar-Arr' dying away on a long-drawn-out note, came from the direction of the village. So sudden and so unexpected had the scream been that I involuntarily stood up with the intention of slipping down from the tree and dashing up to the village, for the thought flashed through my mind that the man-eater was killing one of my men. Then in a second flash of thought I remembered I had counted them one by one as they had passed my tree, and that I had watched them out of sight on their way back to camp to see if they were obeying my instructions to keep close together.

The scream had been the despairing cry of a human being in mortal agony, and reason questioned how such a sound could have come from a deserted village. It was not a thing of my imagination, for the kakar had heard it and had abruptly stopped barking, and the sambur had dashed away across the fields closely followed by her young one. Two days previously, when I had escorted the men to the village, I had remarked that they appeared to be very confiding to leave their property behind doors that were not even shut or latched, and the Headman had answered that even if their village remained untenanted for years their property would be quite safe, for they were priest5 of Punagiri and no one would dream of robbing them; he added that as long as the tigress lived she was a better guard of their property – if guard were needed – than any hundred men could be, for no one in all that countryside would dare to approach the village, for any purpose, through the dense forests that surrounded it, unless escorted by me as they had been.

The screams were not repeated, and as there appeared to be nothing that I could do I settled down again on my rope seat. At 10 p.m. a kakar that was feeding on the young wheat crop at the lower end of the fields dashed away barking, and a minute later the tigress called twice. She had now left the village and was on the move, and even if she did not fancy having another meal off the buffalo there was every hope of her coming along the path which she had used twice every day for the past few days. With finger on trigger and eyes straining on the path I sat hour after hour until daylight succeeded moon-light, and when the sun had been up an hour, my men returned. Very thoughtfully they had brought a bundle of dry wood with them, and in a surprisingly short time I was sitting down to a hot cup of tea. The tigress may have been lurking in the bushes close to us, or she may have been miles away, for after she had called at 10 p.m. the jungles had been silent.

When I got back to camp I found a number of men

sitting near my tent. Some of these men had come to inquire what luck I had had the previous night, and others had come to tell me that the tigress had called from midnight to a little before sunrise at the foot of the hill, and that all the labourers engaged in the forests and on the new export road were too frightened to go to work. I had already heard about the tigress from my men, who had informed me that, together with the thousands of men who were camped round Chuka, they had sat up all night to keep big fires going.

Among the men collected near my tent was the Headman of Thak, and when the others had gone I questioned him about the kill at Thak on the 12th of the month, when he so narrowly escaped falling a victim to the man-eater.

Once again the Headman told me in great detail how he had gone to his fields to dig ginger, taking his grand-child with him, and how on hearing his wife calling he had caught the child's hand and run back to the house – where his wife had said a word or two to him about not keeping his ears open and thereby endangering his own and the child's life – and how a few minutes later the tigress had killed a man while he was cutting leaves off a tree in a field above his house.

All this part of the story I had heard before, and I now asked him if he had actually seen the tigress killing the man. His answer was no; and he added that the tree was not visible from where he had been standing. I then asked him how he knew that the man had been killed, and he said, because he had heard him. In reply to further questions he said the man had not called for help but had cried out; and when asked if he had cried out once he said, 'No, three times,' and then at my request he gave an imitation of the

man's cry. It was the same – but a very modified rendering – as the screams I had heard the previous night.

I then told him what I had heard and asked him if it was possible for anyone to have arrived at the village accidentally, and his answer was an emphatic negative. There were only two paths leading to Thak, and every man, woman, and child in the villages through which these two paths passed knew that Thak was deserted and the reason for its being so. It was known throughout the district that it was dangerous to go near Thak in day-light, and it was therefore quite impossible for anyone to have been in the village at eight o'clock the previous night.

When asked if he could give any explanation for screams having come from a village in which there could not – according to him – have been any human beings, his answer was that he could not. And as I can do no better than the Headman, it were best to assume that neither the kakar, the sambur, nor I heard those very real screams – the screams of a human being in mortal agony.

IV

When all my visitors, including the Headman, had gone, and I was having breakfast, my servant informed me that the Headman of Sem had come to the camp the previous evening and had left word for me that his wife, while cutting grass near the hut where his mother had been killed, had come on a blood trail, and that he would wait for me near the ford over the Ladhya in the morning. So after breakfast I set out to investigate this trail.

While I was fording the river I saw four men hurrying towards me, and as soon as I was on dry land they told me that when they were coming down the hill above Sem they had heard a tiger calling across the valley on the hill between Chuka and Thak. The noise of the water had prevented my hearing the call. I told the men that I was on my way to Sem and would return to Chuka shortly, and left them.

The Headman was waiting for me near his house, and his wife took me to where she had seen the blood trail the previous day. The trail, after continuing along a field for a short distance, crossed some big rocks, on one of which I found the hairs of a kakar. A little farther on I found the pug-marks of a big male leopard, and while I was looking at them I heard a tiger call. Telling my companions to sit down and remain quiet, I listened, in order to locate the tiger. Presently I heard the call again, and thereafter it was repeated at intervals of about two minutes.

It was the tigress calling, and I located her as being five hundred yards below Thak and in the deep ravine which, starting from the spring under the mango-tree, runs parallel to the path and crosses it at its junction with the Kumaya Chak path.

Telling the Headman that the leopard would have to wait to be shot at a more convenient time, I set off as hard as I could go for camp, picking up at the ford the four men who were waiting for my company to Chuka.

On reaching camp I found a crowd of men round my tent, most of them sawyers from Delhi, but including the petty contractors, agents, clerks, timekeepers, and gang-men of the financier who had taken up the timber and road construction contracts in the Ladhya valley. These men had come to see me in connexion with my stay at Chuka. They informed me that many of the hillmen carrying timber and working on the road had left for their homes that morning and that if I left Chuka on 1 December, as they had heard I intended doing, the entire labour force, including themselves, would leave on the same day; for already they were too frightened to eat or sleep, and no one would dare to remain in the valley after I had gone. It was then the morning of 29 November, and I told the men that I still had two days and two nights and that much could happen in that time, but that in any case it would not be possible for me to prolong my stay beyond the morning of the first.

The tigress had by now stopped calling, and when my servant had put up something for me to eat I set out for Thak, intending, if the tigress called again and I could locate her position, to try to stalk her; and if she did not call again, to sit up over the buffalo. I found her tracks on the path and saw where she had entered the ravine, and though I stopped repeatedly on my way up to Thak and listened I did not hear her again. So a little before sunset I ate the biscuits and drank the bottle of tea I had brought with me, and then climbed into the almond-tree and took my seat on the few strands of rope that had to serve me as a machan. On this occasion the magpies were absent, so I was unable to get the hour or two's sleep the birds had enabled me to get the previous evening.

If a tiger fails to return to its kill the first night it does not necessarily mean that the kill has been abandoned. I have on occasions seen a tiger return on the tenth night and eat what could no longer be described as flesh. On the present occasion, however, I was not sitting over a kill, but over an animal that the tigress had found dead and off which she had made a small meal, and had she not been a man-eater I would not have considered the chance of her returning the second night good enough to justify spending a whole night in a tree when she had not taken sufficient interest in the dead buffalo to return to it the first night. It was therefore with very little hope of getting a shot that I sat on the tree from sunset to sunrise, and though the time I spent was not as long as it had been the previous night, my discomfort was very much greater for the ropes I was sitting on cut into me, and a cold wind that started blowing shortly after moonrise and continued throughout the night chilled me to the bone. On this second night I heard no jungle or other sounds, nor did the sambur and her young one come out to feed on the fields. As daylight was succeeding moonlight I thought I heard a tiger call in the distance, but could not be sure of the sound or of its direction.

When I got back to camp my servant had a cup of tea and a hot bath ready for me, but before I could indulge in the latter – my forty-pound tent was not big enough for me to bathe in – I had to get rid of the excited throng of people who were clamouring to tell me their experiences of the night before. It appeared that shortly after moonrise the tigress had started calling close to Chuka, and after calling at intervals for a couple of hours had gone off in the direction of the labour camps at Kumaya Chak. The men in these camps hearing her coming started shouting to try to drive her away, but so far from having this effect the shouting only infuriated her the more, and she demonstrated in front of the camps until she had cowed the men into silence. Having accomplished this, she spent the rest of the nigh t between the labour camps and Chuka, daring all and sundry to shout at her. Towards morning she had gone away in the direction of Thak, and my informants were surprised and very disappointed that I had not met her.

This was my last day of man-eater hunting, and though I was badly in need of rest and sleep, I decided to spend what was left of it in one last attempt to get in touch with the tigress.

The people not only of Chuka and Sem but of all the surrounding villages, and especially the men from Talia Des where some years previously I had shot three man-eaters, were very anxious that I should try sitting up over a live goat, for, said they, 'All hill tigers eat goats, and as you have had no luck with buffaloes, why not try a goat?' More to humour them than with any hope of getting a shot, I consented to spend this last day in sitting up over the two goats I had already purchased for this purpose.

I was convinced that no matter where the tigress wandered to at night, her headquarters were at Thak, so at midday, taking the two goats, and accompanied by four of my men, I set out for Thak.

The path from Chuka to Thak, as I have already mentioned, runs up a very steep ridge. A quarter of a mile on this side of Thak the path leaves the ridge, and crosses a more or less flat bit of ground which extends right up to the mango-tree. For its whole length across this flat ground the path passes through dense brushwood, and is crossed by two narrow ravines which run east and join the main ravine. Midway between these two ravines, and a hundred yards from the tree I had sat in the previous two nights, there is a giant almond-tree; this tree had been my objective when I left camp. The path passes right under the tree, and I thought that if I climbed half-way up not only should I be able to see the two goats, one of which I intended tying at the edge of the main ravine and the other at the foot of the hill to the right, but I should also be able to see the dead buffalo. As all three of these points were at some distance from the tree, I armed myself with an accurate .275 rifle, in addition to the 450/400 rifle which I took for an emergency.

I found the climb up from Chuka on this last day very trying, and I had just reached the spot where the path leaves the ridge for the flat ground, when the tigress called about a hundred and fifty yards to my left. The ground here was covered with dense undergrowth and trees interlaced with creepers, and was cut up by narrow and deep ravines, and strewn over with enormous boulders – a very unsuitable place in which to stalk a man-eater. However, before deciding on what action I should take, it was necessary to know whether the tigress was lying down, as she very well might be, for it was then 1 p.m., or whether she was on the move and if so in what direction. So making the men sit down behind me I listened, and presently the call was repeated; she had moved some fifty yards, and appeared to be going up the main ravine in the direction of Thak.

This was very encouraging, for the tree I had selected to sit in was only fifty yards from the ravine. After enjoining silence on the men and telling them to keep close behind me, we hurried along the path. We had about two hundred yards to go to reach the tree and had covered half the distance when, as we approached a spot where the path was bordered on both sides by dense brushwood, a covey of kaleege pheasants rose out of the brushwood and went screaming away. I knelt down and covered the path for a few minutes, but as nothing happened we went cautiously forward and reached the tree without further incident. As quickly and as silently as possible one goat was tied at the edge of the ravine, while the other was tied at the foot of the hill to the right; then I took the men to the edge of the cultivated land and told them to stay in the upper veranda of the Headman's house until I fetched them, and ran back to the tree. I climbed to a height of forty feet, and pulled the rifle up after me with a cord I had brought for the purpose. Not only were the two goats visible from my seat, one at a range of seventy and the other at a range of sixty yards, but I could also see part of the buffalo, and as the .275 rifle was very accurate I felt sure I could kill the tigress if she showed up anywhere on the ground I was overlooking.

The two goats had lived together ever since I had purchased them on my previous visit, and, being separated now, were calling lustily to each other. Under normal conditions a goat can be heard at a distance of four hundred yards, but here the conditions were not normal, for the goats were tied on the side of a hill down which a strong wind was blowing, and even if the tigress had moved after I had heard her, it was impossible for her not to hear them. If she was hungry, as I had every reason to believe she was, there was a very good chance of my getting a shot.

After I had been on the tree for ten minutes a kakar barked near the spot the pheasants had risen from. For a minute or two my hopes rose sky-high and then dropped back to earth, for the kakar barked only three times and ended on a note of inquiry; evidently there was a snake in the scrub which neither he nor the pheasants liked the look of.

My seat was not uncomfortable and the sun was pleasingly warm, so for the next three hours I remained in the tree without any discomfort. At 4 p.m. the sun went down behind the high hill above Thak, and thereafter the wind became unbearably cold. For an hour I stood the discomfort, and then decided to give up, for the cold had brought on an attack of ague, and if the tigress came now it would not be possible for me to hit her. I re-tied the cord to the rifle and let it down, climbed down myself and walked to the edge of the cultivated land to call up my men.

V

There are few people, I imagine, who have not experienced that feeling of depression that follows failure to accomplish anything they have set out to do. The road back to camp after a strenuous day when the chukor bag is full is only a step compared with the same road which one plods over, mile after weary mile, when the bag is empty, and if this feeling of depression has ever assailed you at the end of a single day, and when the quarry has only been chukor, you will have some idea of the depth of my depression that evening when, after calling up my men and untying the goats, I set off on my two-mile walk to camp, for my effort had been not of a single day or my quarry a few birds, nor did my failure concern only myself.

Excluding the time spent on the journeys from and to home, I had been on the heels of the man-eater from 23 October to 7 November, and again from 24 to 30 November, and it is only those of you who have walked in fear of having the teeth of a tiger meet in your throat who will have any idea of the effect on one's nerves of days and weeks of such anticipation.

Then again my quarry was a man-eater, and my failure to shoot it would very gravely affect everyone who was working in, or whose homes were in, that area. Already work in the forests had been stopped, and the entire population of the largest village in the district had abandoned their homes. Bad as the conditions were they would undoubtedly get worse if the man-eater was not killed, for the entire labour force could not afford to stop work indefinitely, nor could the population of the surrounding villages afford to abandon their homes and their cultivation as the more prosperous people of Thak had been able to do.

The tigress had long since lost her natural fear of human beings, as was abundantly evident from her having carried away a girl picking up mangoes in a field close to where several men were working, killing a woman near the door of her house, dragging a man off a tree in the heart of a village, and, the previous night, cowing a few thousand men into silence. And here was I, who knew full well what the presence of a man-eater meant to the permanent and to the temporary inhabitants and to all the people who passed through the district on their way to the markets at the foothills or the temples at Punagiri, plodding down to camp on what I had promised others would be my last day of man-eater hunting; reason enough for a depression of soul which I felt would remain with me for the rest of my days. Gladly at that moment would I have bartered the success that had attended thirty-two years of man-eater hunting for one unhurried shot at the tigress.

I have told you of some of the attempts I made during this period of seven days and seven nights to get a shot at the tigress, but these were by no means the only attempts I made. I knew that I was being watched and followed, and every time I went through the two miles of jungle between my camp and Thak I tried every trick I have learnt in a lifetime spent in the jungles to outwit the tigress. Bitter though my disappointment was, I felt that my failure was not in any way due to anything I had done or left undone.

VI

My men when they re-joined me said that, an hour after the kakar had barked, they had heard the tigress calling a long way off, but were not sure of the direction. Quite evidently the tigress had as little interest in goats as she had in buffaloes, but even so it was unusual for her to have moved at that time of day from a locality in which she was thoroughly at home, unless she had been attracted away by some sound which neither I nor my men had heard; however that may have been, it was quite evident that she had gone, and as there was nothing further that I could do I set off on my weary tramp to camp.

The path, as I have already mentioned, joins the ridge that runs down to Chuka a quarter of a mile from Thak, and when I now got to this spot where the ridge is only a few feet wide and from where a view is obtained of the two great ravines that run down to the Ladhya River, I heard the tigress call once and again across the valley on my left. She was a little above and to the left of Kumaya Chak, and a few hundred yards below the Kot Kindri ridge on which the men working in that area had built themselves grass shelters.

Here was an opportunity, admittedly forlorn and unquestionably desperate, of getting a shot; still it was an opportunity and the last I should ever have, and the question was, whether or not I was justified in taking it.

When I got down from the tree I had one hour in which to get back to camp before dark. Calling up the men, hearing what they had to say, collecting the goats, and walking to the ridge had taken about thirty minutes, and judging from the position of the sun, which was now casting a red glow on the peaks of the Nepal hills, I calculated I had roughly half an hour's daylight in hand. This time factor, or perhaps it would be more correct to say light factor, was all-important, for if I took the opportunity that offered, on it would depend the lives of five men.

The tigress was a mile away, and the intervening ground

was densely wooded, strewn over with great rocks and cut up by a number of deep nullahs, but she could cover the distance well within the half-hour – if she wanted to. The question I had to decide was, whether or not I should try to call her up. If I called and she heard me, and came while it was still daylight and gave me a shot, all would be well; on the other hand, if she came and did not give me a shot some of us would not reach camp, for we had nearly two miles to go, and the path the whole way ran through heavy jungle, and was bordered in some places by big rocks, and in others by dense brushwood. It was useless to consult the men, for none of them had ever been in a jungle before coming on this trip, so the decision would have to be mine. I decided to try to call up the tigress.

Handing my rifle over to one of the men, I waited until the tigress called again and, cupping my hands round my mouth and filling my lungs to their utmost limit, sent an answering call over the valley. Back came her call and thereafter, for several minutes, call answered call. She would come, had in fact already started, and if she arrived while there was light to shoot by, all the advantages would be on my side, for I had the selecting of the ground on which it would best suit me to meet her. November is the mating season for tigers, and it was evident that for the past forty-eight hours she had been rampaging through the jungles in search of a mate, and that now, on hearing what she thought was a tiger answering her mating call, she would lose no time in joining him.

Four hundred yards down the ridge the path runs for fifty yards across a flat bit of ground. At the far right-hand side of this flat ground the path skirts a big rock and then drops steeply, and continues in a series of hairpin bends, down to the next bench. It was at this rock I decided to meet the tigress, and on my way down to it I called several times to let her know I was changing my position, and also to keep in touch with her.

I want you now to have a clear picture of the ground in your mind, to enable you to follow the subsequent events. Imagine then a rectangular piece of ground forty yards wide and eighty yards long, ending in a more or less perpendicular rock face. The path coming down from Thak runs on to this ground at its short or south end, and after continuing down the centre for twenty-five yards bends to the right and leaves the rectangle on its long or east side. At the point where the path leaves the flat ground there is a rock about four feet high. From a little beyond where the path bends to the right, a ridge of rock, three or four feet high, rises and extends to the north side of the rectangle, where the ground falls away in a perpendicular rock face. On the near or path side of this low ridge there is a dense line of bushes approaching to within ten feet of the four-foot-high rock I have mentioned. The rest of the rectangle is grown over with trees, scattered bushes, and short grass.

It was my intention to lie on the path by the side of the rock and shoot the tigress as she approached me, but when I tried this position I found it would not be possible for me to see her until she was within two or three yards, and further, that she could get at me either round the rock or through the scattered bushes on my left without my seeing her at all. Projecting out of the rock, from the side opposite to that from which I expected the tigress to approach, there was a narrow ledge. By sitting sideways I found I could get a little of my bottom on the ledge, and by putting my left hand flat on the top of the rounded rock and stretching out my right leg to its full extent and touching the ground with my toes, retain my position on it. The goats and men I placed immediately behind, and ten to twelve feet below me.

The stage was now set for the reception of the tigress, who while these preparations were being made had approached to within three hundred yards. Sending out one final call to give her direction, I looked round to see if my men were all right.

The spectacle these men presented would under other circumstances have been ludicrous, but was here tragic. Sitting in a tight little circle with their knees drawn up and their heads together, with the goats burrowing in under them, they had that look of intense expectancy on their screwed-up features that one sees on the faces of spectators waiting to hear a big gun go off. From the time we had first heard the tigress from the ridge, neither the men nor the goats had made a sound, beyond one suppressed cough. They were probably by now frozen with fear – as well they might be – and even if they were, I take my hat off to those four men who had the courage to do what I, had I been in their shoes, would not have dreamt of doing. For seven days they had been hearing the most exaggerated and blood-curdling tales of this fearsome beast that had kept them awake the past two nights, and now, while darkness was coming on, and sitting unarmed in a position where they could see nothing, they were listening to the man-eater drawing nearer and nearer; greater courage, and greater faith, it is not possible to conceive.

The fact that I could not hold my rifle, a D.B. 450/400, with my left hand (which I was using to retain my precarious seat on the ledge) was causing me some uneasiness, for apart from the fear of the rifle's slipping on the rounded top of the rock – I had folded my handkerchief and placed the rifle on it to try to prevent this – I did not know what would be the effect of the recoil of a high-velocity rifle fired in this position. The rifle was pointing along the path, in goat legs I took the .275 rifle from the man who was holding it, rammed a clip of cartridges into the magazine and sent a stream of five bullets singing over the valley and across the Sarda into Nepal. Two shots, to the thousands of men in the valley and in the surrounding villages who were anxiously listening for the sound of my rifle, might mean anything, but two shots followed by five more, spaced at regular intervals of five seconds, could only be interpreted as conveying one message, and that was, that the man-eater was dead.

I had not spoken to my men from the time we had first heard the tigress from the ridge. On my telling them now that she was dead and that there was no longer any reason for us to be afraid, they did not appear to be able to take in what I was saying, so I told them to go up and have a look while I found and lit a cigarette. Very cautiously they climbed up to the rock, but went no farther for, as I have told you, the tigress was touching the other side of it. Late in camp that night, while sitting round a camp-fire and relating their experiences to relays of eager listeners, their narrative invariably ended up with, 'and then the tiger whose roaring had turned our livers into water hit the sahib on the head and knocked him down on top of us and if you don't believe us, go and look at his face'. A mirror is superfluous in camp, and even if I had had one it could not have made the swelling on my jaw, which put me on milk diet for several days, look as large and as painful as it felt.

By the time a sapling had been felled and the tigress lashed to it, lights were beginning to show in the Ladhya valley and in all the surrounding camps and villages. The four men were very anxious to have the honour of carrying the tigress to camp, but the task was beyond them; so I left them and set off for help.

In my three visits to Chuka during the past eight months I had been along this path many times by day and always with a loaded rifle in my hands, and now I was stumbling down in the dark, unarmed, my only anxiety being to avoid a fall. If the greatest happiness one can experience is the sudden cessation of great pain, then the second greatest happiness is undoubtedly the sudden cessation of great fear. One short hour previously it would have taken wild elephants to have dragged from their homes and camps the men who now, singing and shouting, were converging from every direction, singly and in groups, on the path leading to Thak. Some of the men of this rapidly growing crowd went up the path to help carry in the tigress, while others accompanied me on my way to camp, and would have carried me had I permitted them. Progress was slow, for frequent halts had to be made to allow each group of new arrivals to express their gratitude in their own particular way. This gave the party carrying the tigress time to catch us up, and we entered the village together. I will not attempt to describe the welcome my men and I received, or the scenes I witnessed at Chuka that night, for having lived the greater part of my life in the jungles I have not the ability to paint word-pictures.

A hayrick was dismantled and the tigress laid on it, and an enormous bonfire made from driftwood close at hand to light up the scene and for warmth, for the night was dark and cold with a north wind blowing. Round about midnight my servant, assisted by the Headman of Thak and

Kunwar Singh, near whose house I was camped, persuaded the crowd to return to their respective villages and labour camps, telling them they would have ample opportunity of feasting their eyes on the tigress the following day. Before leaving himself, the Headman of Thak told me he would send word in the morning to the people of Thak to return to their village. This he did, and two days later the entire population returned to their homes. and have lived in peace ever since.

After my midnight dinner I sent for Kunwar Singh and told him that in order to reach home on the promised date I should have to start in a few hours, and that he would have to explain to the people in the morning why I had gone. This he promised to do, and I then started to skin the tigress. Skinning a tiger with a pocket-knife is a long job, but it gives one an opportunity of examining the animal that one would otherwise not get, and in the case of man-eaters enables one to ascertain, more or less accurately, the reason for the animal's having become a man-eater.

The tigress was a comparatively young animal and in the perfect condition one would expect her to be at the beginning of the mating season. Her dark winter coat was without a blemish, and in spite of her having so persistently refused the meals I had provided for her she was encased in fat. She had two old gunshot wounds, neither of which showed on her skin. The one in her left shoulder, caused by several pellets of homemade buckshot, had become septic, and when healing the skin, over quite a large surface, had adhered permanently to the flesh. To what extent this wound had incapacitated her it would have been difficult to say, but it had evidently taken a very long time to heal, and could quite reasonably have been the cause of her having become a man-eater. The second wound, which was in her right shoulder, had also been caused by a charge of buckshot, but had healed without becoming septic. These two wounds received over kills in the days before she had become a man-eater were quite sufficient reason for her not having returned to the human and other kills I had sat over.

After having skinned the tigress I bathed and dressed, and though my face was swollen and painful and I had twenty miles of rough going before me, I left Chuka walking on air, while the thousands of men in and around the valley were peacefully sleeping.

I have come to the end of the jungle stories I set out to tell you, and I have also come near the end of my man-eater hunting career.

I have had a long spell and count myself fortunate in having walked out on my own feet and not been carried out on a cradle in the manner and condition of the man of Thak.

There have been occasions when life has hung by a thread and others when a light purse and disease resulting from exposure and strain have made the going difficult, but for all these occasions I am amply rewarded if my hunting has resulted in saving one human life.

www.ingramcontent.com/pod-product-compliance
Lightning Source LLC
Chambersburg PA
CBHW020326170426

43200CB00006B/284